How SAS Works

A Comprehensive Introduction to the SAS System

Paul A. Herzberg
York University

Second edition

Springer-Verlag

Captus Press

Sole distributors in all countries and territories except Canada
Springer-Verlag New York Inc.
175 Fifth Avenue
New York, NY10010
USA

Sole distributors in Canada
Captus Press Inc.
York University Campus
4700 Keele Street
North York, Ontario
M3J 1P3

ISBN 0–387–97291–9   Springer-Verlag New York
ISBN 3–540–97291–9   Springer-Verlag Heidelberg

Canadian Cataloguing in Publication Data

Herzberg, Paul A., 1936–
     How SAS works

2nd ed.
ISBN 0–921801–28–9   (Captus Press)

1. SAS (Computer program).   2. Mathematical
statistics – Data processing.   I. Title.

QA276.4.H47 1990   005.3   C90–093647–9

10 9 8 7 6 5 4 3 2 1
Printed in Canada

CONTENTS IN BRIEF

CONTENTS

SAS TIPS

EXHIBITS

PREFACE

The SAS® System[1] sets the standard for computer analysis of data. The SAS System is available on a wide range of computers. And the SAS System is comprehensive—you can do almost anything from the simplest report to the most complex statistical analysis. But you can only use the SAS System successfully if you know how SAS works. Hence this book.

Chapter 1 provides a brief overview of some of the capabilities of the SAS System, a comparison with competing systems, and a list of some of the computers on which the SAS System can run. But in order to use the SAS System you need more information. The developers of the SAS System, SAS Institute, have done an admirable job of documenting their system. The two principal reference manuals, described in more detail below, total 2,000 pages. I haven't seen all the documentation of the SAS System but it probably totals several times that.

This massive documentation is primarily for those who use the SAS System extensively and who are prepared to spend time in preparation. SAS Institute has been less successful in providing an introductory book about their system. In my view, there are two requirements for such a book:

1. the book should provide the information the beginner needs to use the SAS System for small- to medium-size jobs, and

2. the book should provide a model of how SAS works so that you can read the reference documentation after reading the book.

With respect to the first requirement, SAS Institute does publish a *SAS Introductory Guide* but it is too brief; only the most trivial programs can be written with its guidance. However, the second requirement is even more important. The reference manuals that SAS Institute publishes are just that—reference manuals. The reader of these manuals is assumed to have a model of the SAS System so that when you look up, say, a particular statement, you will understand the many features of the SAS System referred to in the description of that statement. The manuals are not written so that you can start at the beginning and build up a model of how SAS works. My experience, and that of many other users of the SAS System, is that we have had to read and re-read the manuals before many terms are understood.

How SAS Works has been written to fill both requirements—for an introduction to the SAS System and for the development of a model of the SAS System in a step-by-step manner. When you have read *How SAS Works* you should be able to get the results you want from the SAS System and, if you want to pursue your study of the SAS System, you should be able to read the reference manuals published by SAS Institute.

I have referred to a "model" several times above. Here are some examples of how my book helps you develop such a model.

• The SAS data set is central to all work in the SAS System. I describe the data set's structure, including the index, which contains information about the characteristics (type, length, format, etc.) of each variable. I show how these characteristics are determined.

---

[1] SAS is a registered trademark of SAS Institute Inc., Cary, NC, USA.

- SAS data sets are usually created in DATA steps. I describe how the DATA step executes. Firm understanding of this process is essential to understanding most SAS programs.

- Formats are one of the SAS System's most useful features. A format is essentially a transformation between an internal and an external representation. Thinking of a format in this way helps explain many apparently puzzling aspects of its use.

- One of the most powerful features of the SAS System is the ease with which subgroup analyses may be carried out. However, in order to specify such analyses you must have a clear understanding of sorting. Subgroup analyses are also closely related to formats since another way to look at formats is as a subgrouping of the values of a variable.

- Many users of the SAS System have been baffled by the "sum" statement. The accumulation of sums in the SAS language is quite different from other programming languages. I believe I have explained the sum statement clearly.

Each of these topics is described in a unified fashion in *How SAS Works*. For each topic, you have to look in many places in the reference manuals to find the same information.

Relation to the SAS User's Guide

The two principal reference manuals published by SAS Institute are the *SAS User's Guide: Basics* and the *SAS User's Guide: Statistics*. *How SAS Works* covers much of the material in *Basics*. After reading *How SAS Works* you should be able to read both *Basics* for more advanced topics not covered here and also *Statistics*, which describes most of the statistical procedures available in the SAS System.

Occasionally, I refer to the *SAS User's Guide* for further information. In any case, it should be understood that I have left out many details in my description, covering only what I consider essential for the beginner. Since my goal is to make the reader expert enough to read the *SAS User's Guide*, I have in almost all cases retained the same terminology as used in that publication.[2]

Syntactic conventions

See Appendix A for the syntactic conventions used in this book. These conventions are essentially those which SAS Institute uses in its publications.

---

[2] I use PROC *procedure* rather than PROC *program*, since I do not aim for the complete generality allowed in the SAS System to execute non-SAS programs. I use END = *endvariable* since the *SAS User's Guide* is inconsistent here. (In the description of the INFILE statement, END = *variable* is used; in the description of the SET statement, END = *name* is used.) I use VALUE *formatname* (instead of *name*) and FORMAT *formatname* (instead of *format*) for consistency. Finally, I use the LINES statement instead of the vestigial CARDS statement for in-stream data.

Generation of exhibits

All the exhibits in the book were generated by the SAS System at the same time as the final formatting of the document (by Waterloo SCRIPT). The exhibits and the programs themselves were incorporated into the document only at that time. Because of this I am confident that the programs do what they are claimed to do and there is almost no chance of error or inconsistency in the exhibits and the programs.

SAS Tips

Seven topics which are somewhat off the main stream of the development of their corresponding chapters are placed at the end of those chapters as "SAS Tips".

Acknowledgements

I have depended on many others during the writing of this book. I could always call on Michael Friendly and Marshal Linfoot for their extensive knowledge of the SAS System and of Waterloo SCRIPT. They also made valuable criticisms of my book at every stage. Elke Weber helped me define the scope and focus of the book. Peter Cribb and Peter Roosen-Runge encouraged me to write the book for a course in which the three of us taught. I am especially grateful to Peter Cribb, the course director, for his support of my book and for his willingness to use it in the course.

Other colleagues, including Arnold Love, Tony Nield, and Uri Shafrir, provided helpful criticism. The students in the course, particularly Janine Weinstock, pointed out sections which were not clear or which were plain wrong.

I have worked closely with Randy Hoffman of Captus Press during the past year and thank him for his enthusiasm for my book. Without his efforts, *How SAS Works* would never have been published. I also want to thank Pauline Lai of Captus Press who gave me much sound advice about the design of the book.

I am, of course, responsible for errors and infelicities which remain.

My wife, Louise, provided the essential foundation of support and encouragement without which I would never have completed the book.

Paul A. Herzberg

Part 1
INTRODUCTION TO THE SAS SYSTEM

Part 1 describes the general structure of the SAS System and how to use the system to create simple reports and statistical summaries. One of the features of the SAS System is the ease with which simple computer tasks can be specified. Yet the same system and language can also be used to specify tasks of considerable complexity, as illustrated in the later parts of this book.

Chapter 1 describes the general structure of the SAS System and SAS programs. This description is somewhat more abstract than is typical of the following chapters. You may wish to skim this materal now and return to it later. Chapter 2 shows a complete example of a SAS job, including data file, program file, print file, and SAS log. For many readers, this chapter will be the best introduction to the SAS System. Chapter 3 is an introduction to the DATA step and to SAS data sets. Chapters 4 and 5 describe a number of SAS procedures, for reporting (tables, charts, and plots) and for describing data (frequencies, sums, means, and other statistics).

Chapter 1 also compares the SAS System to other systems and lists some computers on which the SAS System can be run. These matters may not be of interest to you if you have already decided to use the SAS System on an available computer. However, in order to use the SAS System on your computer you must determine some computer-specific matters such as how to prepare and execute a SAS program. These are briefly discussed in Chapter 1. Otherwise, *How SAS Works* needs only occasionally to refer to computer-specific matters since one of the features of the SAS System is that most of the SAS language is independent of the particular computer on which the SAS System is run.

Chapter 1

WHAT IS THE SAS SYSTEM?

The SAS System is a very large software system for analyzing data. With the SAS System you can

- store, retrieve, and modify data with the aid of a powerful programming language,
- use the built-in SAS procedures to carry out statistical analyses and produce reports in standard format, and
- perform customized analyses and reports using the SAS language.

The SAS System includes procedures for

- printing, charting, and plotting (described in Chapter 4),
- simple statistical analyses such as computing means and frequency distributions (Chapter 5), and
- dozens of other procedures for more complex analyses such as analysis of variance, factor analysis, and regression analysis (not described in this book).

The basic SAS software (called "base SAS software") includes the SAS language and procedures to carry out all the above tasks. Many computer installations obtain additional software products from SAS Institute: for example, SAS/GRAPH® for high-precision graphs of the results of SAS procedures, SAS/ETS® for economic and time series analyses, SAS/AF® for sophisticated interactive applications, and SAS/IML® for complex programs using matrices.[1] Use of these additional products requires a thorough understanding, such as provided in *How SAS Works*, of base SAS software.

Some twenty years ago, before the SAS System (and similar systems) became available, it was difficult to carry out analyses such as those mentioned above. It was a job for specialists. Many programs did exist but they were not incorporated into a single system. In order to carry out a particular analysis, many different programs might have to be used. Each program would have its own requirements for setting up the input data. Hence, much of the work involved writing programs to interface these various programs. In recent years, systems such as the SAS System incorporate all such programs into a single system with common standards for input to each of its components. Complex tasks can easily be programmed, even by non-specialists.

The SAS System was created to provide an integrated system for statistical analysis.[2] A comprehensive system for data and statistical analysis must include comprehensive tools for data management. The designers of the SAS System realized this. The result is that the SAS System is not only the leading system for statistical analysis but it is also an excellent system for more data-oriented applications such as are often carried out in database systems. For this purpose, the SAS language includes statements for editing, subsetting, concatenating, merging,

---

[1] SAS/GRAPH, SAS/ETS, SAS/AF, and SAS/IML are registered trademarks of SAS Institute, Cary, NC, USA.

[2] The name "SAS" originally was an acronym for "Statistical Analysis System"; however, SAS Institute now does not consider "SAS" to be an acronym and discourages the use of "Statistical Analysis System" in connection with the name "SAS". Furthermore, "SAS" is to be used only as an adjective. These wishes, and others expressed by SAS Institute in their style guide, have been respected in *How SAS Works* with one exception: "SAS" is used as a noun in the title of this book!

and updating data files. The great merit of the SAS System is that once data have been input to the system, they are available for any procedure since all procedures accept data in the same form. Furthermore, the output of most procedures can be obtained in the same form so that the results of one analysis can be input to procedures to carry out further analyses.

A COMPARISON OF SAS AND OTHER SYSTEMS

There are of course other systems which have some similarities to the SAS System. These include SPSS®, Minitab®, and BMDP®.[3] Each system has its advocates. It is easier for inexperienced people to get a simple job running in SPSS or Minitab than in the SAS System. SPSS does not have the range and depth of procedures as are available in the SAS System. Minitab is designed for smaller-scale applications (including educational training) than the other systems. BMDP is hard to use and is not an integrated system in the same way as the SAS System. However, there are some statistical procedures included in BMDP which are not available in the SAS System.[4]

Nevertheless, in the author's judgement, the designers of the SAS System have created a superior system for both elementary and complex analyses. One of the reasons for this superiority is the separation of the data management aspects from the analysis aspects of the system. As described more fully below, data is input and modified in DATA steps while analyses are performed in PROC steps. This distinction is blurred to some degree in other systems; for simple jobs this may not matter very much, but for more complex ones it does. Hence the superiority of the SAS System.

Most other systems are designed mainly for numeric data. The SAS System, in contrast, is well designed to handle character data and date/time values. Hence, the SAS System can be used for a much wider range of applications.

Another variation among the systems is the amount and quality of the information available about them. SAS Institute has provided very complete and accurate documentation of the SAS System. However, most users find the scale of this documentation intimidating. The other systems have better information for beginning and intermediate users. *How SAS Works* was written to fill the need for better documentation of the SAS System for these users.

COMPUTERS ON WHICH THE SAS SYSTEM CAN RUN

The SAS System is available for a large range of computers.

microcomputers: IBM® Corp.'s PC XT, PC AT, and PS/2 (and compatibles) under MS-DOS® and PC DOS.[5]

---

[3] SPSS is a registered trademark of SPSS, Inc. Minitab is a registered trademark of Minitab, Inc. BMDP is a registered trademark of BMDP Statistical Software, Inc.

[4] The SAS System includes a procedure to execute any BMDP program; hence one can work within the SAS framework and still take advantage of any unique BMDP programs.

[5] IBM is a registered trademark of International Business Machines Corp. MS-DOS is a registered trademark of Microsoft Corp.

minicomputers: Digital Equipment Corp.'s VAX™ under VMS™, Prime Computer, Inc.'s Prime 50 under PRIMOS®, and Data General Corp.'s ECLIPSE® under AOS/VS.[6]

mainframe computers: IBM Corp.'s 370/30xx/43xx and compatible machines under OS, CMS, and DOS/VSE.

One of the features of the SAS language is that it is largely independent of the particular computer and operating system on which the SAS System is run.   Hence it was possible to write *How SAS Works* without constant reference to various computer-specific matters. However, there are a number of questions about your computer and operating system which you must answer before you can create and run a SAS job.   If you are unfamiliar with your computer you should seek the answers to these questions from local "experts".

▶   See SAS Tip 1: *What you need to know about your computer system* (at the end of the chapter).

SAS JOBS, PROGRAMS, AND DATA FILES

Here is a brief description of the structure of a SAS job, the parts of a SAS program, and the types of data files in the SAS System.   For a concrete example, see Chapter 2.

The SAS job

Many computer software systems carry out processing in the following way:

1.   There is the system itself which resides in the computer.
2.   There are commands to be executed by the system; these commands are stored in a *program file* or are entered interactively.
3.   There are data to be processed by the commands; these data are stored in a *data file* (or data files).
4.   The system is invoked (started) to execute the commands which process the data.
5.   Upon completion of the commands the results of the processing are stored in (new) *data files* and in *print files* or displayed on the terminal screen.   The print files may be sent to a printer in order to obtain the results in hard copy form.

These aspects of computer processing can be illustrated for the SAS System by the following diagram:

---

[6] VAX and VMS are trademarks of Digital Equipment Corp.   PRIMOS is a registered trademark of Prime Computer, Inc.   ECLIPSE is a registered trademark of Data General Corp.

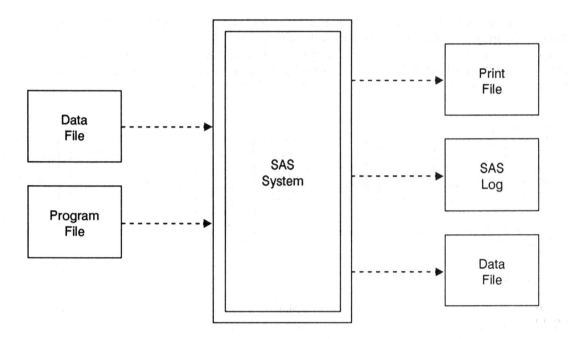

Note that the data files shown on the two sides of the diagram have different roles: the data file on the left is an *input data file*; the one on the right is an *output data file*. The SAS log shown on the right is a special type of print file produced by every run of the SAS System. The SAS log summarizes the commands taken by the SAS System, lists the names of the files produced (either data or print files), and notes any errors which were detected. Not all the files shown are required or produced by every SAS job. Only the program file (or commands entered interactively) is required and only the SAS log is produced by every SAS job. There may be zero, one, or more input data files; there may be zero, one, or more output data files; and there may be zero, one, or more print files (in addition to the SAS log).

We now consider the SAS program and data files in more detail.

The parts of a SAS program

Every SAS program consists of a series of *steps*. Each step is described by one of more statements in the SAS language. There are just two types of steps: DATA steps and PROC steps.

A *DATA step* typically inputs data, modifies the data, and then outputs the data into one or more data files. In short, DATA steps are used to *transform* data.

A *PROC step* invokes one of the many standard procedures available in the SAS System. Each procedure can carry out a particular task on the input data. These tasks vary from simple reports (printing the data) to complex analyses (doing a factor analysis). A PROC step usually outputs its results to the print file but may also create new data files.

A SAS program consists of a chain of these DATA steps and PROC steps. Often the output from one step is input to the next. The following diagram illustrates a SAS program. Note, however, that the sequence of DATA steps and PROC steps can be varied in countless ways. There can be several DATA steps followed by several PROC steps; or the SAS program may have only DATA steps; or the SAS program may have only PROC steps.

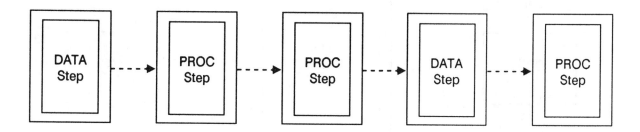

Types of data files

The "data files" referred to above may be of two types: *non-SAS files* and *SAS files*. Non-SAS files can be created and processed by programs outside the SAS System (such as text editors) and can be displayed on the terminal screen and printed. The print file is actually just a particular type of non-SAS file. SAS files are different: they are specially structured data files created by the SAS System (in DATA steps and PROC steps) and can only be processed by the SAS System.

The principal type of SAS file (and the only one discussed in this book) is the *SAS data set*. Much of the power of the SAS System derives from the special structure of the SAS data set. Essentially, SAS data sets are used for the SAS System's internal processing while non-SAS files are used for communication between the SAS System and "the outside world". Input from the outside world to the SAS System is from non-SAS files and output from the SAS System is to non-SAS files (usually print files).

The DATA step is the *only* way to input a non-SAS file to the SAS System. A principal use of the DATA step is to perform such input. However, SAS data sets can also be input to a DATA step. The output from a DATA step is usually one or more SAS data sets but non-SAS files (including print files) can be output from a DATA step. We can illustrate these possibilities by this diagram:

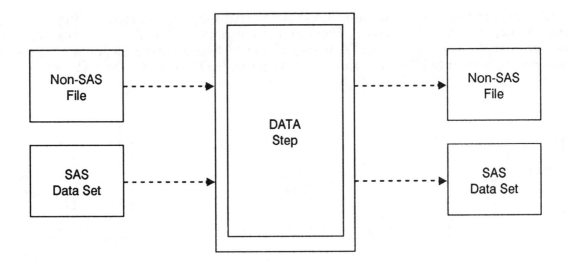

The PROC step is different. The input to a PROC step can only be from a SAS data set.[7] This restriction means that the specification of what the PROC step is to do can usually be very short, since the SAS System can obtain the information it needs about the input file from the special structure of the SAS data set. (Such information would include the names and types of the variables and the number of observations.) PROC steps usually output only a print file but some PROC steps also output a data file in the form of a SAS data set.[8] If another form of output data file is required (i.e., a non-SAS file) it must be created from the output SAS data set by a subsequent DATA step. We illustrate the PROC step in the following diagram:

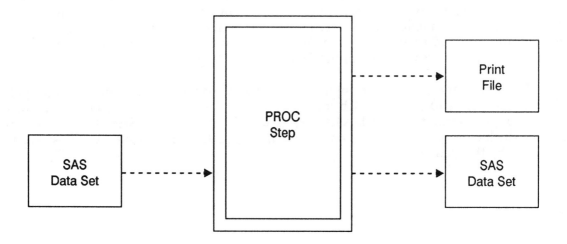

---

[7] There are a few SAS procedures which do not have input from a data file at all. For example, some SAS procedures report on the SAS System itself (e.g., PROC OPTIONS).

[8] There are some SAS procedures which do not output any data file but have some other purpose (e.g., PROC FORMAT).

In summary, PROC steps input and output only SAS data sets (with the exception of the print file) while DATA steps can input and output non-SAS files in addition to SAS data sets. This strong separation between the functions of DATA steps and PROC steps is one of the most important features of the design of the SAS System and the SAS language.

SAS Tip 1   What You Need To Know about Your Computer System

In order use the SAS System on your computer you have to know the answers to the following questions:

How do I use my computer system?

You must know how to use a terminal, what the functions of the various keys on the terminal are, how to log on to your system, and how to create files using a text editor.

How do I create a SAS program?

You must know how to create a SAS program either by a text editor or interactively. If you create a program file by a text editor, you must be aware of any file naming conventions required by your version of the SAS System.

How do I execute a SAS program?

The SAS System provides several ways to execute a SAS program, including interactive and non-interactive modes. Each mode of execution has its own way of accessing the SAS program and of displaying the output data files, including the print file.

How do I define a *fileref*?

The *fileref* is the name given internally in a SAS program to a non-SAS file. This name has to be defined by an operating system statement. The definition creates an association of the *fileref* with the full identification of the file, using the file naming conventions of the particular operating system you are using.

How do I name, save, and access permanent SAS data sets?

The naming, saving, and accessing of permanent SAS data sets requires knowledge of your computer's operating system. Temporary SAS data sets are not usually a problem. All the examples in *How SAS Works* use temporary SAS data sets.

What SAS system options do I have to be aware of?

The SAS System uses a vast array of options, most of which are for specialist use. However, there may be some options you have to be aware of. Examples are LINESIZE, which controls the width of the print file and the SAS log, and DQUOTE, which allows character constants to be bounded by double as well as single quotes.

Chapter 2

A SAS DEMONSTRATION

A typical SAS job processes input data to produce printed output. Two decades ago the input data was usually punched on cards, which were read by a card reader under control of the SAS System. The output from the job was printed on a line printer. In those days, it was perhaps easier for beginners to understand what the computer was doing since you could see the steps: the computer read the cards, did some processing, and printed the results. Now these steps are largely hidden. The input data are keyed into a computer file (usually a disk file). The file is read by the SAS System. The computer then carries out some processing of the data and places the results in another computer file, called the print file. This print file can be viewed on a terminal screen or can be sent to a printer if hard copy is desired. It is essential for the user of a modern computer system such as the SAS System to have a good understanding of computer files: how to create them and how to modify, view, and print them.

In this chapter we describe a complete example of a SAS job. The input data are stored in a *data file*. The processes we wish to carry out are described by a *SAS program* which is stored in a *program file*. We call upon the SAS System to execute the SAS program. During execution of the SAS program, two new files are created: the *print file* and the *SAS log*. These files and their relation to the SAS System are shown below. Note that the arrows indicate which of the files are input to and which are output from the SAS System.

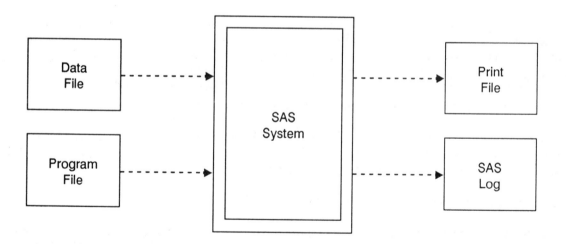

The following sections describe each of the four files associated with the SAS job.

THE DATA FILE

The data for the example in this chapter (and for a number of examples in the rest of the book) are a subset of the data in Hodges, J. L., Krech, D., & Crutchfield, R. S. (1975). *Statlab: An empirical introduction to statistics.* New York: McGraw Hill. In brief, the data are of families consisting of mother, father, and one child. Data for the child were obtained at birth and at age ten years. The latter date is referred to as the "test" date. See the Statlab book for further information about the study itself and more detail about the variables. In order to be processed by the SAS System the data are stored in a file. This file has 72 records, one record for each family. (A record can be thought of as a line in the file.) The file is shown in Exhibit 2.1. Each record consists (in this file) of 42 columns or characters, some of which are blank. The information in the record is grouped into fields of one or more columns. Each field represents one variable. The definitions of the Statlab variables (and the columns which they occupy) are shown in Exhibit 2.2.[1]

From these exhibits we see, for example, that the first record is for the family with identification code "11-21". The child is female, has blood type B and Rh+, was 21.0 inches and 7.1 pounds at birth, was 53.1 inches and 72 pounds at age ten years, is right-handed, was right-eye dominant on the first occasion and left-eye dominant on the second, and had scores of 81 and 33 on the Peabody and Raven tests. The mother graduated from high school and never smoked.

In order for the SAS System to process the Statlab data, the system must know where the data file is located. This information is specified in various ways depending on the computer's operating system. It is impossible in this book to explain how this is done for even a sampling of possible operating systems. See SAS Tip 1: *What you need to know about your computer system* in Chapter 1. The operating system will define the location of the file by what is known as a *fileref* (file reference). In other words, this *fileref* is a shorthand for the location of the file. Let us assume that the *fileref* is "STATLAB". The *fileref* is used in the SAS program itself to refer to this file. (See next section.)

---

[1] The complete data in the Statlab book consist of 30 variables and 1296 families.

Exhibit 2.1 The Statlab Data File

```
11-21 2 7 21.0   7.1 53.1   72 2   81 33 2   N
11-51 2 5 21.5   7.1 56.1   64 1   63 24 2   N
12-21 2 5 22.0   9.7 55.3   83 1   84 30 3   N
12-51 2 1 21.0   8.9 57.9   69 1   74 33 2  20
13-21 2 7 20.0   6.4 51.1   59 1   66 28 2  20
13-51 2 6 21.0   9.8 52.8   64 1   77 32 1   N
14-21 2 5 18.0   4.9 55.3   67 4   67 24 4   N
14-51 2 6 20.5   7.4 50.0   54 8   84 33 3  10
15-21 2 6 19.0   6.7 52.4   66 1   73 42 2  20
15-51 2 6 20.5   6.9 55.9   91 4   85 34 2   N
16-21 2 9 19.5   6.5 56.8   96 1   97 40 3  10
16-51 2 5 20.0   6.9 52.6   67 8   82 18 2   N
21-21 2 6 20.0   6.9 55.5   69 1   81 12 1  10
21-51 2 6 20.5   7.4 52.8   70 1   77 39 4   N
22-21 2 6 19.5   7.0 53.5   68 4   66 44 2   N
22-51 2 5 21.0   6.9 54.4   78 7   82 44 4   N
23-21 2 5 21.0   8.6 53.2   90 1   67 11 2   N
23-51 2 6 21.0  10.0 53.8   80 8   66 26 2   N
24-21 2 5 22.0  10.0 56.1   97 4   78 33 2   Q
24-51 2 6 21.5   7.5 60.0  100 8   79 42 2  02
25-21 2 1 20.3   6.9 52.6   59 5   82 48 4   N
25-51 2 4 21.0   8.3 54.4   82 5   86 36 4  04
26-21 2 5 21.0   8.3 50.7   60 4   80 28 3   N
26-51 2 5 21.0   7.7 54.9   74 2   78 31 4   Q
31-21 2 5 19.5   6.6 52.0   63 4   75 34 4  12
31-51 2 6 21.3   8.4 51.9   60 2   65 27 3   N
32-21 2 5 20.0   6.6 50.7   54 1   76 22 1  20
32-51 2 7 20.0   6.6 55.0   66 4   74 24 2   N
33-21 2 6 19.5   6.3 48.8   52 1   81 41 4   N
33-51 2 5 22.0   8.2 52.1   58 4   80 43 4   Q
34-21 2 7 21.5   9.1 57.5  108 1   88 21 2  01
34-51 2 3 21.0   8.0 55.2   78 1   74 22 2   N
35-21 2 5 20.5   7.4 51.1   66 8   78 14 3   N
35-51 2 2 19.0   6.4 50.7   56 4   93 24 0   Q
36-21 2 5 19.5   6.5 54.2   78 4   67 35 1   N
36-51 2 9 20.8   6.8 52.6   72 4   84 39 3   N
41-21 1 7 20.5   6.9 50.8   59 4   69 21 1   Q
41-51 1 6 18.5   5.8 55.9   78 5   85 21 1  20
42-21 1 6 20.0   8.5 53.1   71 5   77 20 2   N
42-51 1 6 19.0   6.5 53.5   68 4   82 28 2   N
43-21 1 9 22.0   8.3 53.1   70 8   74 21 3   Q
43-51 1 6 21.0   8.2 53.8   68 1   89 42 3   Q
44-21 1 2 22.0   8.2 52.8   66 1   78 27 3  20
44-51 1 5 20.0   7.5 52.7   70 4   83 25 3   Q
45-21 1 6 19.0   6.4 55.2   76 1   69 33 3   N
45-51 1 5 21.5   8.1 54.1   75 1   81 21 3  35
```

```
46-21 1 6 22.0  8.8 56.3 62 1 83 27 1  Q
46-51 1 6 21.0  8.8 54.0 69 1 74 28 3  N
51-21 1 7 20.0  5.9 54.1 70 8 78 30 1 30
51-51 1 6 22.0 10.1 56.7 82 2 86 36 2 13
52-21 1 6 20.5  6.5 51.4 60 1 77 26 4  N
52-51 1 5 21.0  8.5 48.9 54 3 83 16 2  Q
53-21 1 9 18.0  5.9 49.8 58 1 71 28 1 35
53-51 1 5 22.5  8.9 54.8 77 3 70 25 3  N
54-21 1 7 20.0  7.4 57.9 92 5 77 15 3 20
54-51 1 5 20.5  7.9 61.1 65 1 68 26 2  N
55-21 1 6 19.5  7.8 54.6 71 4 62 10 2  Q
55-51 1 8 19.0  6.1 56.0 92 1 73 32 2  Q
56-21 1 6 19.0  6.7 50.2 62 1 65 26 3  N
56-51 1 6 21.5  8.2 55.2 72 4 93 34 4 06
61-21 1 6 19.0  6.8 51.3 75 1 65 23 1  N
61-51 1 6 20.0  6.1 57.4 76 4 96 26 3  Q
62-21 1 6 21.5  8.3 53.5 68 1 86 49 2  N
62-51 1 5 18.5  5.1 49.9 54 4 79 23 0  N
63-21 1 5 20.0  5.5 52.5 79 1 78 13 4  N
63-51 1 6 20.5  7.5 54.8 79 1 84 24 4  N
64-21 1 5 22.5  9.9 52.8 69 1 91 37 4  N
64-51 1 9 20.0  7.7 55.9 73 8 81 36 2  N
65-21 1 2 20.0  6.6 55.3 72 2 79 34 1  N
65-51 1 6 21.5  9.3 53.4 68 1 71 37 4  Q
66-21 1 6 21.0  9.5 52.9 64 5 75 17 2  N
66-51 1 2 22.5  8.5 55.4 71 8 60 13 2  N
```

Source: Hodges, J. L., Krech, D., & Crutchfield, R. S. (1975). *Statlab: An empirical introduction to statistics.* New York: McGraw Hill. Reprinted with permission.

Exhibit 2.2 Definitions of the Statlab Variables

Variable	Columns	Definition
FAMILY	1-5	Identification code for the family
SEX	7	Sex of child (1=male; 2=female)
BLOOD	9	Blood type

Code	Meaning	Code	Meaning	Code	Meaning
1	O, Rh−	4	AB, Rh−	7	B, Rh+
2	A, Rh−	5	O, Rh+	8	AB, Rh+
3	B, Rh−	6	A, Rh+	9	unknown

Variable	Columns	Definition
BIRTHLGH	11-14	Length of baby (to tenth of inch)
BIRTHWGT	16-19	Weight of baby (to tenth of pound)
TESTHGT	21-24	Height of child at test (to tenth of inch)
TESTWGT	26-28	Weight of child at test (to nearest pound)
LATERAL	30	Laterality at test measured by a combination of left or right handedness (H), with left or right eyedness (E), the latter being measured on two occasions (E_1 and E_2)

Code	H	E_1	E_2	Code	H	E_1	E_2
1	R	R	R	5	L	R	R
2	R	R	L	6	L	R	L
3	R	L	R	7	L	L	R
4	R	L	L	8	L	L	L

Variable	Columns	Definition
PEABODY	32-34	Score on Peabody Picture Vocabulary Test
RAVEN	36-37	Score on Raven Progressive Matrices Test
MOTHEDUC	39	Education of Mother

Code	Meaning
0	less than grade 8
1	Grade 8 to 12
2	High school graduation
3	Some college
4	College graduation

Variable	Columns	Definition
MOTHSMOK	41-42	Smoking history of Mother (N=never; Q=quit; 01 to 99=number cigarettes/day)

Source: Hodges, J. L., Krech, D., & Crutchfield, R. S. (1975). *Statlab: An empirical introduction to statistics*. New York: McGraw Hill. Reprinted with permission.

THE SAS PROGRAM

Suppose we want to prepare a SAS job that does two tasks: print a table of the values of some of the variables for each family and print a frequency chart of the variable MOTHSMOK (Smoking history of Mother). The frequency chart is a histogram in which the height of each bar represents the number of mothers with a particular smoking history (i.e., never, quit, or number of cigarettes per day). The SAS job is specified by a SAS program which consists of statements stored in a program file (as distinct from the data file). After the program file is created it must be processed or run by the SAS System. How this is done depends on the computer's operating system. We therefore cannot explain here how to run a SAS program on your computer; in this book we only give the SAS programs themselves. See SAS Tip 1: *What you need to know about your computer system* in Chapter 1.

The statements in a SAS program are grouped into *steps*, each step specifying a single task, such as printing a table, or printing a chart. There are two types of steps in a SAS program: DATA steps and PROC steps.

- DATA steps typically read a data file and transform the data into a form suitable for processing by the SAS System.

- PROC steps (PROCedure steps) process the data, producing, for example, tables and charts.

Our program will require three steps:

Step 1   A DATA step to read the STATLAB DATA file and transform the data into a form suitable for the SAS System.

Step 2   A PROC step to print a table of values of selected variables for every family.

Step 3   A PROC step to print a frequency chart of the variable MOTHSMOK.

The program is shown in Exhibit 2.3. The three steps are easy to identify. All DATA steps begin with the DATA statement; all PROC steps begin with a PROC statement which identifies the procedure to be executed.

▶   See SAS Tip 2: *Preparing the SAS program* (at the end of the chapter).

The DATA step

The DATA step in this example consists of the DATA statement followed by two other statements. The INFILE statement specifies the *fileref* of the file where the data are stored. As discussed above, we will assume that the operating system has defined the location of the file by a *fileref* "STATLAB". The INPUT statement specifies the names of the variables in the order in which they appear in each record of the file. Since the values in each record are separated by one or more blank columns, it is not necessary to specify the columns in which the values lie; however, the order of the variables must be correct. Note that two of the variables, FAMILY and MOTHSMOK, are followed by dollar signs ($). The dollar sign is

Exhibit 2.3 SAS Program

```
DATA DEMO;
  INFILE STATLAB;
  INPUT FAMILY $ SEX BLOOD BIRTHLGH BIRTHWGT TESTHGT
      TESTWGT LATERAL PEABODY RAVEN MOTHEDUC MOTHSMOK $;

PROC PRINT DATA=DEMO;
  ID FAMILY;
  VAR SEX BLOOD BIRTHWGT MOTHEDUC MOTHSMOK;

PROC CHART DATA=DEMO;
  VBAR MOTHSMOK;
```

used in an INPUT statement to indicate that the preceding variable is a *character* variable rather than a *numeric* variable. MOTHSMOK has some letters as values; FAMILY has hyphens (special characters) as part of the identification. Numeric variables can only have digits, decimal points, and signs (+ or −) as part of their values. Hence MOTHSMOK and FAMILY must be defined as character variables.

▶   See SAS Tip 3: *Deciding whether a variable is numeric or character* (at the end of
         the chapter).

Once the DATA step has been executed, the Statlab data exist in an internal form suitable for further processing by the SAS System. This internal form is known as a *SAS data set*. Since the DATA statement is

```
DATA DEMO;
```

the *name* of the SAS data set is DEMO, by which it can be referred in the succeeding PROC steps. (SAS data sets are described further in Chapter 3.)

The PROC steps

The first PROC step requests that the PRINT procedure produce a table of values of the variables FAMILY, SEX, BLOOD, BIRTHWGT, MOTHEDUC, and MOTHSMOK for each of the 72 families in the Statlab data. This step has three statements. The first statement is the PROC PRINT statement itself which specifies the procedure (PRINT) to execute and the data set (DEMO) to process. The second statement is an ID statement which ensures that the variable FAMILY is printed first in each line to identify each family.[2] The third statement is a VAR statement listing the variables which are to be printed (in addition to FAMILY) for each family. The variables are printed in the order specified on the VAR statement.

The second PROC step begins with a PROC CHART statement specifying that the CHART procedure is to be used. The PROC statement is followed by a VBAR statement specifying that the chart is to be of the variable MOTHSMOK.

THE PRINT FILE

The output from the two PROC steps is written on the print file which may be viewed on the terminal screen or printed. The PROC PRINT output is shown in Exhibit 2.4; the PROC CHART output is shown in Exhibit 2.5. These exhibits are self-explanatory, illustrating one of the principal virtues of the SAS System: comprehensible and attractive output can be obtained without having to specify more than the bare minimum of information to the SAS System. Note, for example, that in Exhibit 2.5 the SAS System has determined all the possible values of the MOTHSMOK variable and has spaced these values out along the horizontal axis of the chart. Similarly, the SAS System chose a suitable vertical scale for the frequencies of occurrence of each value of MOTHSMOK.

---

[2] If the ID statement were omitted (and FAMILY added to the VAR statement), the output would be similar except that an additional column would appear to the left, labelled "OBS", giving the observation number (1, 2, 3, etc.) of each line in the table. Further details about the statements for the PRINT procedure may be found in Chapter 4.

Exhibit 2.4 PROC PRINT Output

SAS

FAMILY	SEX	BLOOD	BIRTHWGT	MOTHEDUC	MOTHSMOK
11-21	2	7	7.1	2	N
11-51	2	5	7.1	2	N
12-21	2	5	9.7	3	N
12-51	2	1	8.9	2	20
13-21	2	7	6.4	2	20
13-51	2	6	9.8	1	N
14-21	2	5	4.9	4	N
14-51	2	6	7.4	3	10
15-21	2	6	6.7	2	20
15-51	2	6	6.9	2	N
16-21	2	9	6.5	3	10
16-51	2	5	6.9	2	N
21-21	2	6	6.9	1	10
	. . . .				
55-21	1	6	7.8	2	Q
55-51	1	8	6.1	2	Q
56-21	1	6	6.7	3	N
56-51	1	6	8.2	4	06
61-21	1	6	6.8	1	N
61-51	1	6	6.1	3	Q
62-21	1	6	8.3	2	N
62-51	1	5	5.1	0	N
63-21	1	5	5.5	4	N
63-51	1	6	7.5	4	N
64-21	1	5	9.9	4	N
64-51	1	9	7.7	2	N
65-21	1	2	6.6	1	N
65-51	1	6	9.3	4	Q
66-21	1	6	9.5	2	N
66-51	1	2	8.5	2	N

Note: The ellipsis points (. . .) denote observations deleted to save space.

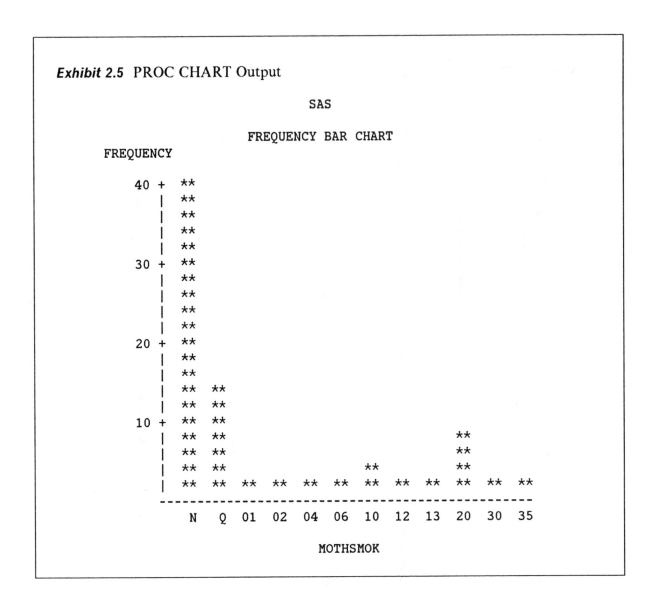

Exhibit 2.5 PROC CHART Output

THE SAS LOG

The objective of our example SAS job was the print file containing the output from the two PROC steps. The SAS System always produces another file, called the SAS log. This file displays the SAS program which was processed, shows any errors which the SAS System found, and notes the result of each DATA and PROC step.

Exhibit 2.6 shows the SAS log for the example program of this chapter. The first few lines give the date and information about the version of the SAS System and the computer on which the job was run. The first program line shows the operating system statement used to

Exhibit 2.6 The SAS Log for Program in Exhibit 2.3

```
1           SAS(R) LOG   CMS SAS 5.18      VM/CMS CMS USER HERZBERG
                                           18:05 SUNDAY, AUGUST 6, 1989


NOTE: COPYRIGHT (C) 1984,1986 SAS INSTITUTE INC., CARY, N.C.  27
512, U.S.A.
NOTE: CMS SAS RELEASE 5.18 AT YORK UNIVERSITY (07019005).

NOTE: CPUID   VERSION = FF  SERIAL = 010858  MODEL = 4381 .

  1 cms filedef statlab disk statlab data *;
  2   DATA DEMO;
  3     INFILE STATLAB;
  4     INPUT FAMILY $ SEX BLOOD BIRTHLGH BIRTHWGT TESTHGT
  5         TESTWGT LATERAL PEABODY RAVEN MOTHEDUC MOTHSMOK $;
  6
  7


NOTE: INFILE STATLAB IS FILE STATLAB DATA H1
NOTE: 72 LINES WERE READ FROM INFILE STATLAB.
NOTE: DATA SET WORK.DEMO HAS 72 OBSERVATIONS AND 12 VARIABLES.
NOTE: THE DATA STATEMENT USED 0.16 SECONDS AND 96K.

  7   PROC PRINT DATA=DEMO;
  8     ID FAMILY;
  9     VAR SEX BLOOD BIRTHWGT MOTHEDUC MOTHSMOK;
 10
 11
NOTE: THE PROCEDURE PRINT USED 0.21 SECONDS AND 96K
      AND PRINTED PAGES 1 TO 2.

 11   PROC CHART DATA=DEMO;
 12     VBAR MOTHSMOK;
NOTE: THE PROCEDURE CHART USED 0.17 SECONDS AND 96K
      AND PRINTED PAGE 3.
NOTE: SAS USED 96K MEMORY.

NOTE: SAS INSTITUTE INC.
      SAS CIRCLE
      PO BOX 8000
      CARY, N.C. 27512-8000
```

define the *fileref* "STATLAB".[3] The next four lines are the statements of the DATA step, followed by notes about the execution of the step. Similarly each of the PROC steps is followed by summary notes.

EXERCISES

1.   Describe all the characteristics of the family in the Statlab data with identification code "44–51".

2.   For the operating system of your computer determine:

     a.   How to define the *fileref* for a file;

     b.   How to process a SAS program by the SAS System.

---

[3] This SAS job, as all others in this book, was run in the CMS operating system. In that system, as in others, the statement needed to define the *fileref* can be included in the SAS program. Note that in other operating systems, this statement would be different.

SAS Tip 2 Preparing the SAS Program

A SAS program consists of a series of SAS statements. Each statement is terminated by a semi-colon. Usually one writes one statement on each line of the program file, but this is not necessary. A statement may extend over more than one line or, indeed, several statements may be written on one line. However, if a statement is split over more than one line it must be split between two words—a word itself cannot be split. Statements may be written in upper- or lowercase. Here are some statements illustrating these points:

```
PROC PRINT
      DATA=
      DEMO;
   ID FAMILY; VAR SEX BLOOD BIRTHWGT MOTHEDUC MOTHSMOK;

   PROC CHART data=demo;vbar mothsmok;
```

Even though there is great flexibility allowed in how statements are placed in a program file, programmers have found that it pays to follow certain conventions, such as:

- Separate each step in the SAS program by a blank line.
- Indent all statements after the first statement in each step.
- If a statement is split over several lines, indent all lines after the first.
- Use comments to explain and document a lengthy program or to explain unusual aspects of the program.

Exhibit 2.3 illustrates the first three of these conventions.

Comments can be inserted in programs in two ways. You can use the *comment statement*:

   message;

Any message placed between the asterisk and the semi-colon will be ignored by the SAS System. The message can extend over several lines of the SAS program. (However, the message cannot contain a semi-colon!) Alternatively, comments can be inserted at any place in a program (but not breaking up a word) by preceding and following the message by special markers:

   /**message**/

Note that this form of a comment is not, itself, a SAS statement. Here are some examples of comments:

```
   * Checking variables X, Y, Z ;
   DATA TEST;
      INFILE DATA1;  /* Old data file */
      INPUT X Y Z;

   PROC PRINT DATA=TEST;
```

SAS Tip 3 Deciding Whether a Variable Is Numeric or Character

It may seem simple to decide whether a variable is numeric or character: the values of numeric variables must be numbers, i.e., only digits, or digits and a decimal point, possibly preceded by a sign. If the variable isn't numeric it must be character. However, there are other considerations which should be made when SAS programs are planned.

The difficulty arises with variables whose values are numbers, but the numbers are essentially codes. Consider the variable MOTHEDUC in the Statlab data. Its values are certainly numbers (0, 1, 2, 3, 4), but these are codes for various levels of education. It would be nonsensical to calculate an average of this variable or to carry out other numerical calculations. In this sense, the variable MOTHEDUC is more like a character than a numerical variable.

In the Statlab data, the variables BIRTHLGH, BIRTHWGT, TESTHGT, TESTWGT, PEABODY, and RAVEN are "true" numeric variables on which numeric calculations can sensibly be done. These variables should certainly be defined as numeric in any SAS program. As was noted in the chapter, the variables FAMILY and MOTHSMOK must certainly be defined as character in a SAS program since they contain letters or special characters (hyphens) in some of the values. This leaves the variables SEX, BLOOD, LATERAL, and MOTHEDUC which seem to be numeric but whose values actually are codes. These variables can be defined to be either numeric or character, since character variables don't *have* to have non-digits as values. *The distinguishing characteristic of a character variable is that no calculations are performed on the values*—the values are just treated as strings of characters.

Whether one defines such variables as numeric or character is largely a matter of style and personal choice, but one must be aware of the implications of the choice that is made. Here are some considerations:

1. Some SAS procedures (such as PROC MEANS in Chapter 5) automatically analyze *all* numeric variables in a data set unless the user specifies which variables to analyze. If a variable, such as BLOOD in the Statlab data, were defined as numeric, then one would have to specifically exclude it from an analysis by procedures such as PROC MEANS. However, if the variable were defined as character, no special action would need to be taken.

2. Some procedures (in particular PROC CHART) work with both numeric and character variables, but require special options when numeric variables which have only a few values (such as MOTHEDUC) are charted. See the discussion of the DISCRETE option with PROC CHART in Chapter 4 and also its use with a format in Chapter 12.

3. In many SAS programs a variable is compared to specific values. This occurs in PROC FORMAT (Chapter 12) and in logical expressions (Chapter 8). If the variable is numeric, the specific value is written as a number; if the variable is character, the specific value must be written in quotes. For example, in a VALUE statement used in PROC FORMAT, for a numeric variable one might write:

    VALUE 1 = 'Male' . . .

However, if the variable is defined as character, one must write:

```
VALUE '1' = 'Male' . . .
```

Unless one is careful, one might omit the quotes around the number; the resulting error messages are often difficult to diagnose. If the variable were defined as numeric, the problem would not arise. Somewhat similar considerations apply to logical expressions, although in this case the SAS System takes default actions (converting numeric to character or vice versa) and gives a warning message on the SAS log.

The first two points are arguments in favour of defining numerically coded variables as character; the last is an argument in favour of defining such variables as numeric. In this book, the author has usually defined such variables as numeric.

Chapter 3

THE DATA STEP AND SAS DATA SETS

In Chapter 2 we have seen that a SAS job consists of a series of statements divided into DATA steps and PROC steps. DATA steps are typically used to input and modify data. PROC steps are typically used to perform calculations and print results. This separation of tasks into two types of steps is very helpful to both the beginner and the expert in planning and creating a SAS job.

In this chapter we describe the DATA step in more detail. The following two chapters describe a number of procedures which can be used in PROC steps.

TYPES OF DATA FILES

The procedures specified in PROC steps can process only data stored in a SAS data set. Hence it is necessary to convert data, existing in a non-SAS file, into a special SAS file, called a SAS data set. Simple DATA steps, such as described in this chapter, do just this.

The following diagram summarizes the types of data files discussed in this chapter:

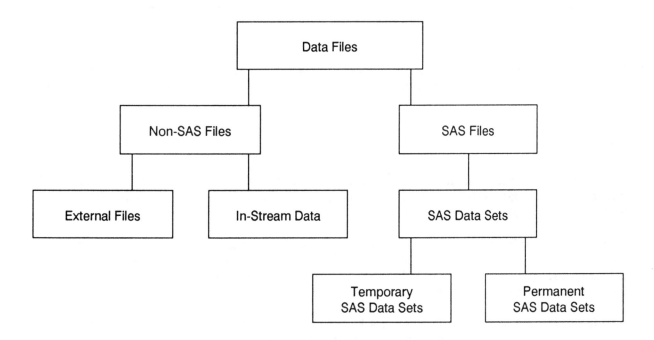

Data files are of two types: non-SAS files and SAS files. As previously noted, only SAS data sets can be processed by procedures in PROC steps. SAS data sets are one type of SAS file; SAS files can only be created by the SAS System. On the other hand, non-SAS files are usually created by a text editor, outside the SAS System. These files are then read by a

DATA step in a SAS program; the result of the DATA step is a SAS data set (i.e., the original data converted to a form that can be processed by further program steps).

Non-SAS files

Data can be stored in two ways in a non-SAS file. Most generally, data would be stored in a separate file, called an *external file* (i.e., external to the SAS System). But for certain purposes it is convenient to include the data together with the SAS program in the program file. Such data are referred to as *in-stream data*. Hence there are two ways to store data in non-SAS files: in an external file or within the program file as in-stream data. The only difference is the physical location of the data.

Most of this chapter is concerned with the reading of a non-SAS file by the DATA step. But first we describe SAS data sets, which are created by DATA steps.

SAS data sets

There are two types of SAS data sets: temporary and permanent. Temporary data sets exist only for the duration of the SAS job and are erased at its termination. Permanent data sets are stored permanently on a disk or tape and remain after the job is terminated. In this book we only discuss temporary data sets since the naming of permanent data sets is more complex and one usually has to write operating system statements to ensure that the permanent data sets are properly saved.

Even though temporary data sets are files, they only exist during the SAS job. Hence you will not see them in any listing of your files. In this respect (as in others) they are quite unlike non-SAS files.

SAS NAMES

For obvious reasons, most objects created in the SAS System must have a name. In particular, SAS data sets and variables have names. These names must follow the rules for what are known as *SAS names*.

SAS names may be single words of from 1 to 8 characters, the first of which must be a letter (A to Z) or an underscore (_). The characters after the first may be letters, digits (0 to 9), or underscores. Note that the SAS System generates certain names including underscores for itself so that, in general, it is best to avoid using underscores in names.

The following are legal variable names: ALPHA, A1234, Z, ZZZZZZZZ, A_B1. The following are not legal: 1A (can't start with a digit), A12345678 (too long), AB$ (illegal character).

THE STRUCTURE OF A DATA STEP

The typical DATA step reads a non-SAS file and creates a SAS data set. The non-SAS file must be located and the method of reading the characters in each record specified. The SAS data set must be given a name so it can be referred to in later steps of the SAS job. These three requirements are specified by three SAS statements:

- *Naming the data set.* The DATA statement (the first statement of the DATA step) specifies the name of the SAS data set to be created by the DATA step.

- *Locating the file.* The location of an external file is specified by an INFILE statement in the DATA step. Alternatively, in-stream data are preceded by a LINES statement in the DATA step.

- *Reading the characters in a record.* The INPUT statement specifies where on the input record each value that is to be read is located.

These three requirements and their associated statements are discussed in the next three sections, respectively.

THE DATA STATEMENT

The DATA step begins, in the simplest cases, with the DATA statement:

    DATA *SASdataset*;

where *SASdataset* is the name to be given to the data set created in the DATA step. The form of the name depends on whether the data set is to be temporary or permanent. The name of a temporary data set is any legal SAS name (see earlier in this chapter). Internally, the SAS System refers to such a data set by a two-level name obtained by preceding the name by "WORK.". For example, if you give the name MYDATA to a data set, the SAS System will refer to that data set by the full name "WORK.MYDATA". As previously mentioned, the naming of permanent data sets is more complex (the name consists of two SAS names separated by a period). Such data sets are not referred to in this book since their use usually requires operating system statements.

▶   See SAS Tip 4: *Does the SAS data set have to be named?* (at the end of the chapter).

LOCATING THE NON-SAS FILE

When the SAS System was first created in the 1970s, the most common form of computer input was cards. Both the data and the SAS statements were punched on cards and both were included in the DATA step. The data cards were preceded by a CARDS statement to distinguish them from the SAS statements. The CARDS statement still remains in the SAS System even though physical cards have almost disappeared. We will use the modern form of the CARDS statement, the LINES statement. Data lines may be included in a DATA step by preceding them with a LINES statement, illustrated below. These data lines are referred to as "in-stream data".

More commonly one prepares data in a separate file (usually a disk file) and indicates to the SAS System where this file is located. The location of such an external file is specified by an INFILE statement. There are many advantages to using the INFILE statement rather than the LINES statement. One of them is that there is a clear distinction between the program (the DATA and PROC steps) and the data (the disk file referred to by the INFILE statement). When the LINES statement is used, the data and program are mixed together. However, for small sets of data it may be more convenient to include the data in the DATA step by a LINES statement since the complications of the INFILE statement and the associated operating system statement are avoided.

The INFILE statement

The INFILE statement has the form:

INFILE *fileref*;

where *fileref* (file reference) identifies the input file. However, *fileref* is not the full identification of the file for the operating system of the computer you are using. The full identification, which serves to locate the file on your computer, usually consists of several parts (file name, file type or extension, etc.). The computer job must include another statement (not a SAS statement, but an operating system statement) which associates the *fileref* with the full identification of the file. See SAS Tip 1: *What you need to know about your computer system* in Chapter 1.

Example

Consider the data lines shown in Exhibit 3.1. If these lines were stored in a file which was to be processed by a DATA step, both an INFILE statement and an operating system statement would be required to read the data. The DATA step might be:

```
DATA SCORES;
   INFILE TESTDATA;
   INPUT X Y Z LASTN $ ;
```

The operating system statement (not shown) would associate the *fileref* TESTDATA with the actual location of the external file. (The INPUT statement is explained later in this chapter.)

It may be puzzling why this complicated method of accessing external files is used by the SAS System. The *fileref* ("TESTDATA" in the above example) could, perhaps, be replaced on the INFILE statement by the full identification of the file. Then only one statement would be needed and the *fileref* would not be required. However, there are good reasons for having a separate operating system statement. Consider what happens if you want to run the job on another computer system. The SAS statements (in the DATA step) would not have to be changed; the only change would be in the operating system statement. Many SAS programs are hundreds or thousands of statements long. The INFILE statement allows for a clear separation of operating system details from the SAS program itself.

Exhibit 3.1 Data Lines To Be Stored Either in an External File or as In-stream Data

```
23 46 5 Smith
32 -77 234 Jones
4 4 88 Arnold
0 70 80 Beatty
18 27 888 Vaughan
```

The LINES statement

The previous example consists of a small set of data with only five observations. Instead of storing the data as an external file it would be easier, in this case, to include the data directly in the program file as in-stream data. See Exhibit 3.2.

Exhibit 3.2 A DATA Step with the LINES Statement

```
DATA SCORES;
   INPUT X Y Z LASTN $ ;
   LINES;
23 46 5 Smith
32 -77 234 Jones
4 4 88 Arnold
0 70 80 Beatty
18 27 888 Vaughan
;
```

Note two matters illustrated by this example. First, the LINES statement (and its following data lines) must *follow* all other statements in the DATA step. Recall that the INFILE statement precedes the INPUT statement. If there is no INFILE statement preceding the INPUT statement, the SAS System expects a LINES statement at the end of the DATA step. Second, the data lines are followed by a line with just a ";" in it. This line is called a *null statement* and identifies the end of the data.[1]

---

[1] Strictly speaking, a null statement is not required if another SAS statement (such as a PROC statement) follows the data lines, provided that the following statement itself includes a semi-colon. However, it seems more logical (and is much safer) to always mark both the beginning *and the end* of in-stream data by the LINES and null statements, respectively.

The Null statement

The semi-colon terminates all SAS statements. When it is used by itself the semi-colon is called the null statement. The principal use of the null statement is to mark the end of a set of data lines as described above.

READING EACH RECORD IN A NON-SAS FILE

The records in a non-SAS file are read by an INPUT statement. This statement serves three principal purposes:

1.   The INPUT statement gives a *name* to each variable which is read.

2.   The INPUT statement states the *type* (character or numeric) of each variable.

3.   The INPUT statement gives the *location* on each record in which each variable is to be found.

Variable names

The names which can be given to variables follow the rules for legal SAS names (see earlier in this chapter).

Numeric and character variables

Recall that two of the variables in the Statlab data (FAMILY and MOTHSMOK) have values which are letters or special characters; these are called *character variables*. The remaining variables (e.g., SEX, BLOOD, BIRTHWGT, etc.) have values which are numbers; these are called *numeric variables*. The values of a character variable can be any string of characters, including digits and special characters. The critical distinction between a character and a numeric variable is that calculations can be carried out only on numeric variables. The digits, if any, in a character variable are treated just as any other characters—they can be printed but no calculations on them can be carried out.[2]

The SAS System assumes that variables are numeric unless otherwise specified. A variable is specified to be character by placing a "$" after the variable's name in the INPUT statement.

---

[2] Some variables, such as BLOOD, could reasonably be defined as character variables—see SAS Tip 3: *Deciding whether a variable is numeric or character* in Chapter 2.

The INPUT statement

The INPUT statement is one of the most complex of all SAS statements. Here we discuss only the two forms of the INPUT statement, list input and column input, which handle most situations. Usually the INPUT statement specifies how *one* line (observation) is read.[3]

List input: Suppose that a data line contains the following data (the scale and bars showing every fifth column):

```
----|----|----|----|

23 56.3    4   46.33
```

The set of columns occupied by each of the numbers (23, 56.3, etc.) is called a *field*. Note that in this case the fields are separated by one (or more) blanks. These data can be read using list input by an INPUT statement such as

```
INPUT AGE HEIGHT X1 X2;
```

The four numbers (23, 56.3, 4, 46.33) are referred to using the the four variable names (AGE, HEIGHT, X1, X2), respectively. List input is certainly the easiest way to read data. You simply list the variables in the order they appear on the data line.

Column input: Alternatively, the same data line could be read by column input, in which the columns in which each field lies are specified:

```
INPUT AGE 1-2   HEIGHT 4-7   X1 11   X2 14-18;
```

(Variable AGE is read from columns 1 to 2, etc.; the single-column field for X1 is specified as just "11" although it could be specified as "11–11".) In this case list input is quite satisfactory and simpler to set up than column input. However, data are sometimes stored in a data line without intervening blanks. Then it is impossible for the SAS System to know where one variable's field stops and the next one starts without a specification of these fields. In such cases column input is required. For example, if the data line is:

```
----|----|----|----|

2356.3446.33
```

then the data could be read by

```
INPUT AGE 1-2   HEIGHT 3-6   X1 7   X2 8-12;
```

This statement specifies that the variable AGE is found in columns 1 to 2, variable HEIGHT is found in columns 3 to 6, etc.

---

[3] The INPUT statement can be modified to read one observation from more than one data line or to read several observations from one data line. See Chapter 9.

Combining list and column input: In some cases it is convenient (or necessary) to combine list and column input—some of the variables in the INPUT statement are specified by list input and others by column input. For example, suppose you want to input only the variables FAMILY, BLOOD, MOTHEDUC, and MOTHSMOK from the Statlab data file. (The fields in which the Statlab variables lie are listed in Exhibit 2.2.) You could use either of the following INPUT statements (note that the field in column 7 has to be skipped over):

```
INPUT FAMILY $ 1-5 BLOOD 9 MOTHEDUC 39 MOTHSMOK 41-42;
INPUT FAMILY $ BLOOD 9 MOTHEDUC 39 MOTHSMOK;
```

The first statement uses column input exclusively; the second uses column input only for BLOOD and MOTHEDUC—the SAS System can determine where the other two variables lie, since list input reads from consecutive fields.

Reading character variables: As noted previously, character variables are specified by following the name by "$". For example, consider the following data line:

```
----|----|----|----|----|

Smith        2356.3746.33
```

This line could be read by

```
INPUT LASTNAME $ 1-12 AGE 13-14 HEIGHT 15-18 X1 19 X2 20-24;
```

If the "$" were omitted, the SAS System would report an error on attempting to read the data line since it would assume, by default, that LASTNAME is a numeric variable; letters cannot be stored in a numeric variable. Note that the "$" *precedes* the column specifications.

▶   See SAS Tip 5: *Preparing the data file* (at the end of the chapter).

PUTTING THE DATA STEP TOGETHER

In summary, a DATA step which reads from an external file consists of at least three statements:

1. A DATA statement to name the resulting data set;

2. An INFILE statement to locate the external file;[4]

3. An INPUT statement to specify the variables, their types, and their locations on each record of the external file.

(In the case of in-stream data, the INFILE statement is omitted; instead, a LINES statement precedes the data lines and a null statement follows the data lines.)

---

[4] You also usually need an operating system statement. See discussion of the INFILE statement earlier in this chapter.

Example 1

We repeat here the three statements for an earlier example in the chapter.

```
DATA SCORES;
   INFILE TESTDATA;
   INPUT X Y Z LASTN $ ;
```

The DATA step creates a data set named SCORES. The external file has *fileref* TESTDATA. And each record has four fields read by list input into four variables, the last of which is a character variable.

Example 2

Similarly, a complete Statlab example (from Chapter 2) is:

```
DATA DEMO;
   INFILE STATLAB;
   INPUT FAMILY $ SEX BLOOD BIRTHLGH BIRTHWGT TESTHGT
      TESTWGT LATERAL PEABODY RAVEN MOTHEDUC MOTHSMOK $;
```

The DATA step creates a data set named DEMO. The external file has *fileref* STATLAB. And each record has 12 fields read by list input into 12 variables, two of which are character variables.[5]

WHAT HAPPENS IN A DATA STEP?

Simple DATA steps are easy to understand. The external file (or in-stream data following the LINES statement) is read according to the specification given in the INPUT statement. The DATA step is followed by one or more PROC steps to perform some calculations and print the results. The design of the SAS System makes such simple tasks easy to program and easy to understand. However, most work with the SAS System requires a deeper understanding of the DATA step.

The DATA step

The DATA step can be thought of as a process which takes an external file (or data lines following the LINES statement) as input and produces a SAS data set as output. The SAS data set has a special structure which can be analyzed by succeeding PROC steps. The statements for the PROC steps are usually quite simple since the PROCs analyze SAS data sets, whose structure is known to the SAS System.

---

[5] The SAS data set could have also been named STATLAB. This would be convenient (since the external file and the data set are versions of the same data) but perhaps confusing to the reader. The SAS System would have no difficulty with the duplicate names since the *fileref* in the INFILE statement refers to the external file and the name of the data set (*SASdataset*) in the DATA statement refers to the SAS data set.

Occasionally a DATA step will not have an input file or will get its data from a SAS data set. Usually the DATA step produces a SAS data set but it may be set up to produce an external file, or several SAS data sets, or even no output data at all. Some of these possibilities are described in succeeding chapters. For now, think of the DATA step as taking an external file as input and producing a SAS data set as output, as shown in this diagram:

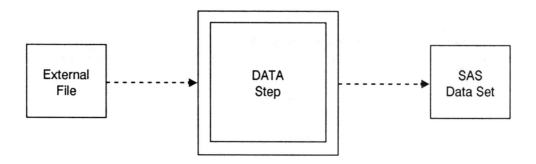

The SAS data set

A SAS data set has two parts. The first part is a two-dimensional table which contains the values of all the variables for each observation. The observations form the rows of the table and the variables form the columns. The second part is an index to the data set. For each variable, the index gives the name of the variable and whether the variable is numeric or character.[6] Exhibit 3.3 illustrates the data set created by the DATA step in Exhibit 3.2.

Further elaboration of the process carried out in a DATA step and of the structure of a SAS data set is found in Part 4.

---

[6] The index contains further characteristics of each variable. These are explained in Chapter 16.

Exhibit 3.3 The SAS Data Set Created by Exhibit 3.2

<u>Table</u>

```
            Variable
               #        1        2        3        4
Observation   ------------------------------------------
    #        |
    1        |         23       46        5     Smith
    2        |         32      -77      234     Jones
    3        |          4        4       88     Arnold
    4        |          0       70       80     Beatty
    5        |         18       27      888     Vaughan
```

<u>Index</u>

```
   Variable        Name      Type
      #        ----------------------
      1              X       numeric
      2              Y       numeric
      3              Z       numeric
      4            LASTN     character
```

SAS Tip 4 Does the SAS Data Set Have To Be Named?

Many SAS jobs, including the simple ones we have illustrated previously, have only one DATA step and hence only one data set. In those jobs it is not necessary to give a name to the data set. (The SAS System assigns a default name, "WORK.DATA1".) All the PROC steps refer to this data set. For example, the SAS job of Chapter 2 could be written:

```
DATA;
   INFILE STATLAB;
   INPUT FAMILY $ SEX BLOOD BIRTHLGH BIRTHWGT TESTHGT
       TESTWGT LATERAL PEABODY RAVEN MOTHEDUC MOTHSMOK $;

PROC PRINT;
   ID FAMILY;
   VAR SEX BLOOD BIRTHWGT MOTHEDUC MOTHSMOK;

PROC CHART;
   VBAR MOTHSMOK;
```

The two PROC steps automatically refer to the most recently created data set, namely the data set created in the DATA step.

However, more complex jobs, particularly those involving several data sets, must have names for the data sets so that the data set required by a PROC step can be specified.

Although there is some saving of effort in using the default name for a SAS data set created in a DATA step, there is considerable merit in naming *every* data set created in a SAS job. There is less potential for confusion and error if that practice is followed. We will name all SAS data sets in this book.

SAS Tip 5 Preparing the Data File

A typical external file (or in-stream data in the DATA step itself) contains a number of lines, one line for each observation. The INPUT statement describes how *one* line is read. Each line is read by the same INPUT statement. Hence, for column input, all lines must be prepared with fields in the same columns. An example of a file in which all lines are prepared in this way is the Statlab data file in Exhibit 2.1.

This restriction does not apply to list input since the fields are separated by blank columns. There must be the same number of fields on each line but in list input these fields could be in different columns on different lines. Exhibit 3.1 illustrates such data lines. Even though the fields are not lined up, the records can be read by the following INPUT statement:

```
INPUT X Y Z LASTN $ ;
```

Note that each record has four fields, the first three of which are numeric and the fourth is character.

It is most important to plan the INPUT statement before creating a data file. It is safest to leave blanks between fields even if the fields are lined up. Then you can use either column or list input (or a combination). The blanks can be inserted into the file by tabbing. However, for large files it may be more convenient (and less likely to produce errors) to create the file without blanks between fields. In this case the fields *must* be lined up and column input used.

Chapter 4

SOME SAS REPORTING PROCEDURES

There are over 60 procedures in base SAS software. In this book we discuss only a few since the *SAS User's Guide* is the best source for detailed information about them. The procedures may be grouped into four categories: reporting, descriptive, utility, and statistics.

- The *reporting* procedures produce simple listings, charts, and plots of SAS data sets. In this chapter we discuss some features of three reporting procedures: PRINT, CHART, and PLOT.

- The *descriptive* procedures perform basic statistical calculations and present the results in tables or simple charts. Chapter 5 discusses three descriptive procedures: FREQ, MEANS, and UNIVARIATE. Some statistical calculations which can be done by PROC CHART are also discussed.

- Among the large number of *utility* procedures in base SAS software are two which are used in many SAS programs: SORT and FORMAT. These are discussed in Part 3.

- The SAS System is well known for its *statistics* procedures, including regression analysis, analysis of variance, factor analysis, etc. They are not discussed in this book, except for the few descriptive procedures mentioned above.

THE PROC STATEMENT

Every PROC step begins with a PROC statement which specifies the name of the procedure to be executed and the name of the SAS data set to be processed by the procedure. The general form of the PROC statement is:

PROC *procedure* DATA = *SASdataset*;

where *procedure* is the name of the procedure desired (e.g., PRINT) and *SASdataset* is the name of the data set to be processed. As discussed in Chapter 3, the name depends on whether the data set is temporary or permanent. A temporary data set has one name (a SAS name); a permanent data set has a double name (two SAS names separated by a period).

THE PROC STEP

Let us begin our discussion of reporting procedures by an example similar to the example in Chapter 2. The new example consists of one DATA step and one PROC step:

```
DATA DEMO;
  INFILE STATLAB;
  INPUT FAMILY $ SEX BLOOD BIRTHLGH BIRTHWGT TESTHGT
       TESTWGT LATERAL PEABODY RAVEN MOTHEDUC MOTHSMOK $;

PROC PRINT DATA=DEMO;
  VAR FAMILY SEX BLOOD BIRTHWGT MOTHEDUC MOTHSMOK;
```

The output from this example is shown in Exhibit 4.1. The output in Exhibit 4.1 differs slightly from that in Exhibit 2.4. Each line begins with the observation number. As noted in more detail in the next section, the observation numbers appear in PROC PRINT output unless an ID statement is used (as it was in the program in Exhibit 2.3).

The processes carried out by the SAS System in this example can be summarized in a diagram:

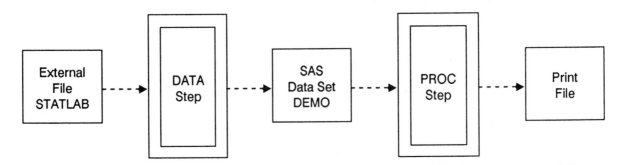

Note that both the program and the diagram indicate the names of the external file (STATLAB) and the SAS data set (DEMO). STATLAB is the *fileref*, defined in an operating system statement (not shown) and referred to in the INFILE statement; DEMO is the *SASdataset*, defined in the DATA statement and referred to in the PROC PRINT statement.

Most SAS jobs can be represented in a similar diagram. The DATA step produces a SAS data set, usually from an input external file (but sometimes from other SAS data sets). The SAS data set produced from the DATA step is then input to the PROC step which generates an output file which can be printed. In this chapter and the next, we will concentrate on the PROC step; hence we can reduce the diagram to:

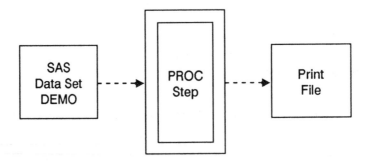

It is not our concern in these chapters how the SAS data set was produced—it might have been produced by a preceding DATA step or it might be a permanent SAS data set. If the SAS data set is permanent, we don't have to have a DATA step in our program at all.

Exhibit 4.1 Selected Variables from Data Set DEMO

SAS

OBS	FAMILY	SEX	BLOOD	BIRTHWGT	MOTHEDUC	MOTHSMOK
1	11-21	2	7	7.1	2	N
2	11-51	2	5	7.1	2	N
3	12-21	2	5	9.7	3	N
4	12-51	2	1	8.9	2	20
5	13-21	2	7	6.4	2	20
6	13-51	2	6	9.8	1	N
7	14-21	2	5	4.9	4	N
8	14-51	2	6	7.4	3	10
9	15-21	2	6	6.7	2	20
10	15-51	2	6	6.9	2	N
11	16-21	2	9	6.5	3	10
12	16-51	2	5	6.9	2	N
13	21-21	2	6	6.9	1	10
			. . . . . .			
57	55-21	1	6	7.8	2	Q
58	55-51	1	8	6.1	2	Q
59	56-21	1	6	6.7	3	N
60	56-51	1	6	8.2	4	06
61	61-21	1	6	6.8	1	N
62	61-51	1	6	6.1	3	Q
63	62-21	1	6	8.3	2	N
64	62-51	1	5	5.1	0	N
65	63-21	1	5	5.5	4	N
66	63-51	1	6	7.5	4	N
67	64-21	1	5	9.9	4	N
68	64-51	1	9	7.7	2	N
69	65-21	1	2	6.6	1	N
70	65-51	1	6	9.3	4	Q
71	66-21	1	6	9.5	2	N
72	66-51	1	2	8.5	2	N

Note: The ellipsis points (. . .) denote observations deleted to save space.

PROC PRINT

The most frequently used procedure in base SAS software is undoubtedly PROC PRINT. The PRINT procedure creates output showing the values of all (or selected) variables for all observations in the input data set. The PROC step begins with the statement:

PROC PRINT DATA = *SASdataset*;

where *SASdataset* is the input data set. The PROC PRINT statement may, optionally, be followed by one or more of the statements:

VAR *variables*;
ID *variables*;
SUM *variables*;

These statements may appear in any order in the PROC step.

The VAR statement

If the VAR statement is used, only those variables listed in the statement are printed and they are printed in the order shown in the statement. (If neither a VAR nor an ID statement is used, all the variables in the data set are printed but they are printed in the order in which they were originally input in the DATA step.)

The ID statement

If the ID statement is used, the variables listed in the statement are printed as the first variables on the left of the page and the observation number is not printed. Both ID and VAR statements may be used in which case the ID variables are followed by the VAR variables. If the ID statement is used alone, all variables are printed, with the ID variables appearing first.

The SUM statement

The variables listed in the SUM statement, if used, are totalled. The totals appear after the last observation. Variables to be totalled need not be specified on the VAR statement; they are, in effect, added to the VAR statement. ID variables cannot be totalled.

Example

Some data (reproduced from Exhibits 3.1 and 3.2) are inputted and printed by the following SAS job:

```
DATA SCORES;
  INPUT X Y Z LASTN $ ;
  LINES;
23 46 5 Smith
32 -77 234 Jones
4 4 88 Arnold
0 70 80 Beatty
18 27 888 Vaughan
;

PROC PRINT DATA=SCORES;
```

Note that the data set is named in the DATA statement and that the PROC PRINT statement includes DATA = SCORES to specify this data set. The resulting output is shown in Exhibit 4.2. The first column is "OBS", the observation number. Each of the other columns is headed by the variable name. This table is essentially the table part of the SAS data set (see Exhibit 3.3).

Exhibit 4.2 A Simple PROC PRINT

```
                          SAS

          OBS     X       Y       Z      LASTN

           1      23      46       5     Smith
           2      32     -77     234     Jones
           3       4       4      88     Arnold
           4       0      70      80     Beatty
           5      18      27     888     Vaughan
```

Suppose we want to print only three of the variables, with LASTN serving to identify each observation, and that we want to total variable Y. We would use the PROC step:

```
PROC PRINT DATA=SCORES;
  ID LASTN;
  VAR Z Y;
  SUM Y;
```

whose output is shown in Exhibit 4.3. Note the absence of the "OBS" column, the ordering of the variables in the order specified on the VAR statement, and the totalling of variable Y.

Exhibit 4.3 A Modified PROC PRINT

```
                        SAS

              LASTN        Z        Y

              Smith        5       46
              Jones      234      -77
              Arnold      88        4
              Beatty      80       70
              Vaughan    888       27
                                  ===
                                   70
```

THE TITLE STATEMENT

All the preceding examples of procedure output have the simple title line "SAS". You can specify your own title line (or several lines) to appear on the output pages. The TITLE statement has the form:

    TITLE '*title*';

The title (following the word "TITLE") in the statement must be bounded by quotes; use either single quotes or double quotes but be consistent—if you use a single quote at the beginning, use a single quote at the end. In the following example we use the TITLE statement and the ID statement (but no VAR statement):

```
PROC PRINT DATA=SCORES;
   TITLE 'Score Output with a Title';
   ID LASTN;
```

All variables are printed, with the ID variable identifying each line. The output is shown in Exhibit 4.4.

Additional title lines can be specified by the statements:

    TITLE*n* '*title*';

where *n*, immediately following "TITLE", can be a digit from 2 to 10, specifying the title line number. ("TITLE1" is the first line and is equivalent to using "TITLE" alone.) For example, these TITLE statements would produce four title lines, the third of which is blank (since there is no TITLE3 statement):

```
Exhibit 4.4

                    Score Output with a Title

            LASTN        X        Y        Z

            Smith       23       46        5
            Jones       32      -77      234
            Arnold       4        4       88
            Beatty       0       70       80
            Vaughan     18       27      888
```

```
TITLE 'Summary of Test Data';
TITLE2 'First Run';
TITLE4 'Experimental Group';
```

Titles may be different in different PROC steps. However, unless changed, the titles, once defined, are carried on from one step to the next. In other words, the TITLE statement is global in scope and is not a statement (like VAR and ID) associated with a particular PROC step. For example, if you want a single title to identify all output from a job, you might place the TITLE statement *before* the first PROC. However, if you want different titles for each PROC, then each TITLE statement must appear *after* the PROC statement to which it applies.

To suppress all titles (and to restore the default "SAS"), use the statement:

    TITLE;

To suppress all titles from line *n* and beyond, use the statement:

    TITLE*n*;

▶   See SAS Tip 6: *Using the TITLE statement* (at the end of the chapter).

PROC CHART

The CHART procedure creates charts of many kinds. In this chapter we explain how to produce vertical bar charts of frequencies by the following statements:

    PROC CHART DATA = *SASdataset*;
        VBAR *variables | options*;

where *SASdataset* is the input data set and *variables* are the names of one or more variables in that data set for which charts are desired. Alternative forms of these charts are specified by the *options* which follow the stroke "/". The stroke is used on many SAS statements to indicate the beginning of statement options.[1] The options may be specified in any order following the stroke.

The CHART procedure can produce other types of charts. Vertical bar charts of means (and sums) are described in Chapter 5. Horizontal bar charts (HBAR), pie charts (PIE), star charts (STAR), and block charts (BLOCK) are not described in this book but are produced by statements whose keyword (as just given in parentheses) is used instead of the keyword VBAR used for vertical bar charts.

Specifying the type of chart (TYPE= option)

The bar charts produced by PROC CHART can be of one of four types:

- TYPE=FREQ produces a frequency chart: frequencies for each value (or interval) of the variable.

- TYPE=PERCENT produces a percentage chart: each frequency is divided by the total number of observations and multiplied by 100.

- TYPE=CFREQ produces a cumulative frequency chart: each bar represents the frequency for that value (or interval) of the variable plus the frequencies for all values (or intervals) to the left.

- TYPE=CPERCENT produces a cumulative percentage chart: the cumulative frequencies are converted to percentages.

The option "TYPE=FREQ" need not be specified since it is the default if no TYPE= option is given.

A frequency chart (the default) of the variable MOTHSMOK was displayed in Exhibit 2.5. This was a chart of a character variable; it displayed the number of observations with each value of MOTHSMOK. We now display a series of charts of the numeric variable MOTHEDUC. A frequency chart of MOTHEDUC is shown in Exhibit 4.5. It was produced by the following statements:

```
DATA REPORT;
  INFILE STATLAB;
  INPUT SEX 7 BIRTHLGH 11-14 BIRTHWGT 16-19
        TESTHGT 21-24 TESTWGT 26-28 MOTHEDUC 39 ;

PROC CHART DATA=REPORT;
  TITLE 'Frequency Chart of Education of Mother';
  VBAR MOTHEDUC / DISCRETE;
```

[1] If no options are requested the stroke should be omitted.

For completeness, we show in the above SAS program the DATA step that creates the data set REPORT. We could have used the data set DEMO (which contains all the Statlab variables) created earlier in the chapter, but, for variety, we create a new data set containing only the variables needed in the illustrations of PROCs CHART and PLOT which follow. Also note that the DISCRETE option has been used in the VBAR statement. The DISCRETE option is explained in the next subsection.

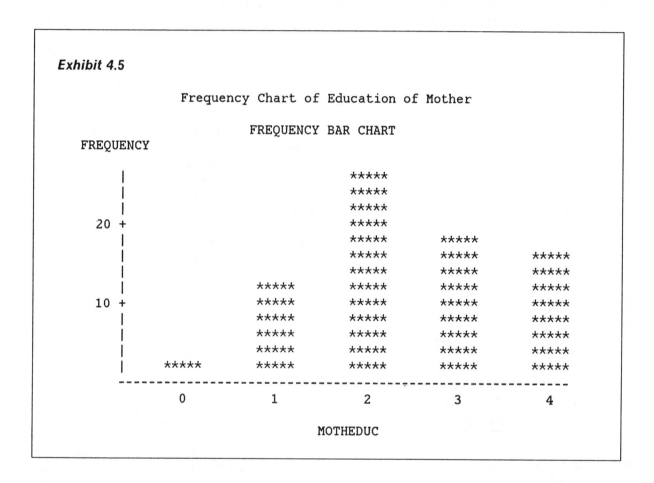

A cumulative frequency chart of MOTHEDUC is shown in Exhibit 4.6. It was produced by the following statements:

```
PROC CHART DATA=REPORT;
   TITLE 'Cumulative Frequency Chart of Education of Mother';
   VBAR MOTHEDUC / DISCRETE TYPE=CFREQ;
```

A percentage chart of MOTHEDUC is shown in Exhibit 4.7. It was produced by the following statements:

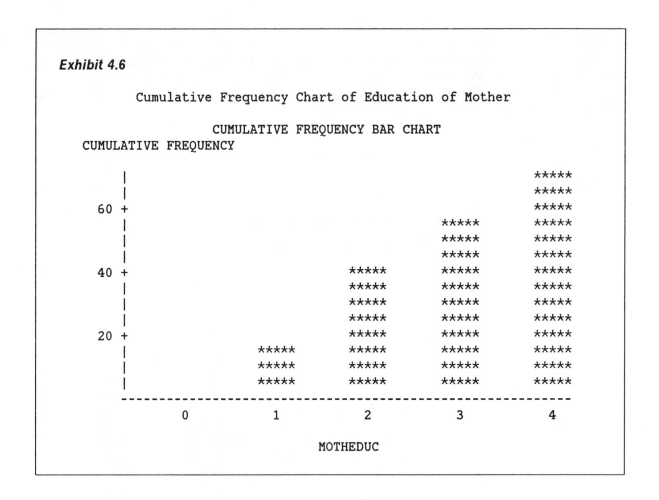

Exhibit 4.6

Cumulative Frequency Chart of Education of Mother

CUMULATIVE FREQUENCY BAR CHART

CUMULATIVE FREQUENCY

```
          |                                                    *****
          |                                                    *****
      60 +                                                     *****
          |                                         *****      *****
          |                                         *****      *****
          |                                         *****      *****
      40 +                              *****        *****      *****
          |                              *****        *****      *****
          |                              *****        *****      *****
          |                              *****        *****      *****
      20 +                              *****        *****      *****
          |                  *****      *****        *****      *****
          |                  *****      *****        *****      *****
          |                  *****      *****        *****      *****
          ----------------------------------------------------------------
                 0            1           2            3           4

                                   MOTHEDUC
```

```
PROC CHART DATA=REPORT;
  TITLE 'Percentage Chart of Education of Mother';
  VBAR MOTHEDUC / DISCRETE TYPE=PERCENT;
```

Exhibit 4.7 (a percentage chart) is the same as Exhibit 4.5 (a frequency chart) except for the scaling of the vertical axis.

Specifying the intervals

PROC CHART assumes that a numeric variable is continuous, unless told otherwise. If no other indication is given to the PROC, it will divide the numeric variable into a convenient number of intervals. *If a division into intervals is desired*, it is usually more satisfactory to specify how this division is to be done (by the MIDPOINTS= or LEVELS= options—see below). *If no division into intervals is desired*, (i.e., the numeric variable has only a few values and you want frequencies for each value) then you must specify the DISCRETE option to prevent PROC CHART from grouping the variable.

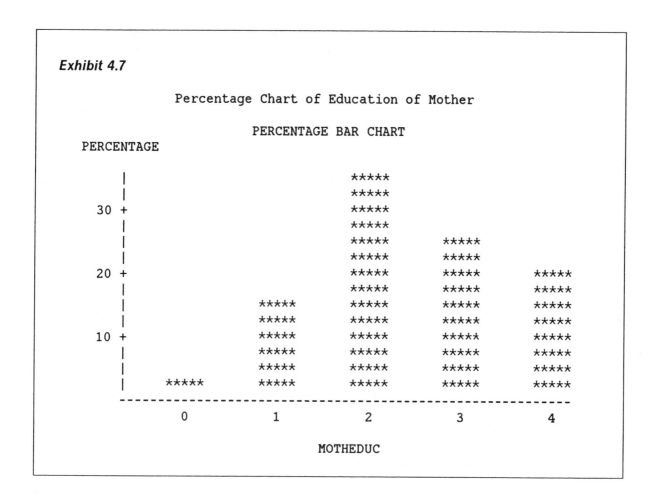

Exhibit 4.7

Percentage Chart of Education of Mother

PERCENTAGE BAR CHART

```
PERCENTAGE

        |                              *****
        |                              *****
     30 +                              *****
        |                              *****
        |                              *****     *****
        |                              *****     *****
     20 +                              *****     *****     *****
        |                              *****     *****     *****
        |                    *****     *****     *****     *****
        |                    *****     *****     *****     *****
     10 +                    *****     *****     *****     *****
        |                    *****     *****     *****     *****
        |                    *****     *****     *****     *****
        |          *****     *****     *****     *****     *****
        ----------------------------------------------------------------
             0         1         2         3         4

                              MOTHEDUC
```

Refer to SAS Tip 3: *Deciding whether a variable is numeric or character* in Chapter 2, where it is noted that there is some advantage to defining a variable which has only a few values as character (rather than numeric) so that you don't have to be concerned about the DISCRETE option.

DISCRETE option: Use this option for a numeric variable if you want to use each value of the variable as a separate interval (bar). No division of values into intervals is to occur. Refer to the preceding three exhibits and the statements which produced them. The variable MOTHEDUC has only five (numeric) values. To prevent PROC CHART dividing these values into intervals, the DISCRETE option must be used. See below (Exhibit 4.9) for an illustration of what happens when DISCRETE is omitted.

MIDPOINTS= option: One way to request division of a variable into intervals is to specify the midpoints of each interval. Exhibit 4.8 was produced by these statements:

```
PROC CHART DATA=REPORT;
   TITLE 'Frequency Chart of Birth Weight';
   VBAR BIRTHWGT / MIDPOINTS=5.5 6.5 7.5 8.5 9.5 10.5 11.5;
```

Since BIRTHWGT is a numeric variable with many values, it is best to specify the intervals. See below (Exhibit 4.10) for an illustration of what happens when the intervals are not specified.

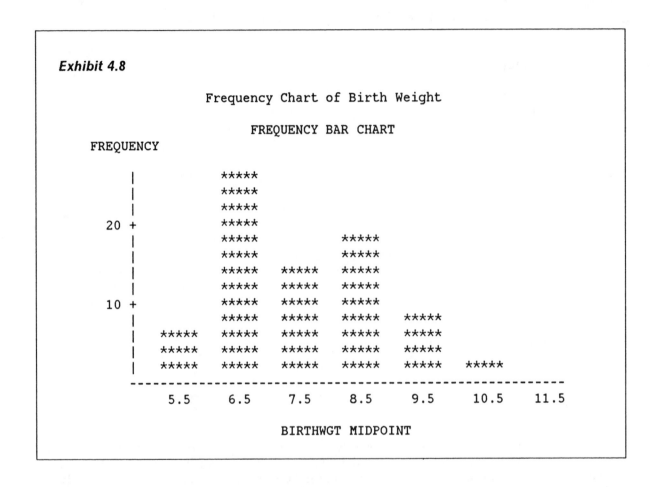

```
Exhibit 4.8

                    Frequency Chart of Birth Weight

                        FREQUENCY BAR CHART
   FREQUENCY

          |           *****
          |           *****
          |           *****
     20  +           *****
          |           *****            *****
          |           *****            *****
          |           *****    *****   *****
          |           *****    *****   *****
     10  +           *****    *****   *****
          |           *****    *****   *****   *****
          |   *****   *****    *****   *****   *****
          |   *****   *****    *****   *****   *****
          |   *****   *****    *****   *****   *****   *****
          -------------------------------------------------------
              5.5     6.5     7.5     8.5     9.5    10.5    11.5

                        BIRTHWGT MIDPOINT
```

LEVELS= option: Another way to specify the division of values into intervals is by the LEVELS= option. Simply specify the number of bars desired. (The term "levels" is used here since the variable has been divided into a number of levels.) For example, to give the same number of bars as before, the VBAR statement could be:

```
VBAR BIRTHWGT / LEVELS=7;
```

However, in this case, PROC CHART still chooses the boundaries and midpoints of the intervals.

Why the intervals should be specified (or DISCRETE used)

In all the previous examples of charts for variable MOTHEDUC (Exhibits 4.5, 4.6, and 4.7), the DISCRETE option was used to prevent the CHART procedure from dividing the variable into intervals. If the DISCRETE option is omitted as in the following PROC step:

```
PROC CHART DATA=REPORT;
   TITLE 'Result for Exhibit 4.5, Omitting DISCRETE';
   VBAR MOTHEDUC;
```

the result is Exhibit 4.9, an unsatisfactory result for a variable with the values 0, 1, 2, 3, and 4.

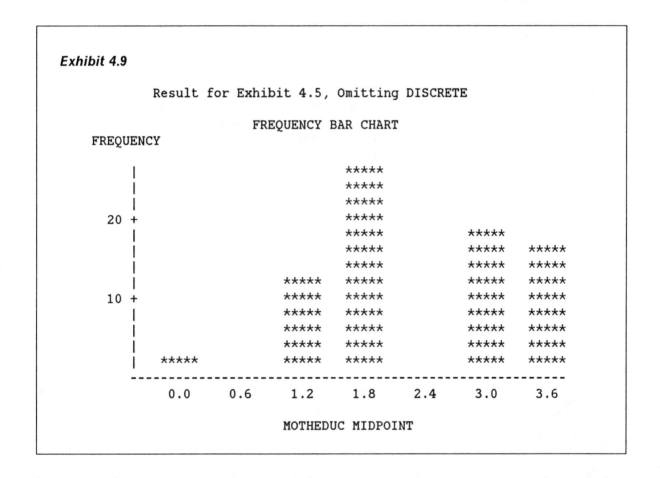

The variable BIRTHWGT is different. It has many values and should be divided into intervals. However, if PROC CHART chooses the intervals the result is not as satisfactory as Exhibit 4.8. If we use the statements

```
PROC CHART DATA=REPORT;
   TITLE 'Result for Exhibit 4.8, Omitting MIDPOINTS=';
   VBAR BIRTHWGT;
```

we get the result in Exhibit 4.10. The intervals are no longer "nice"; their length is 0.6 and the midpoints do not end in .0 or .5.

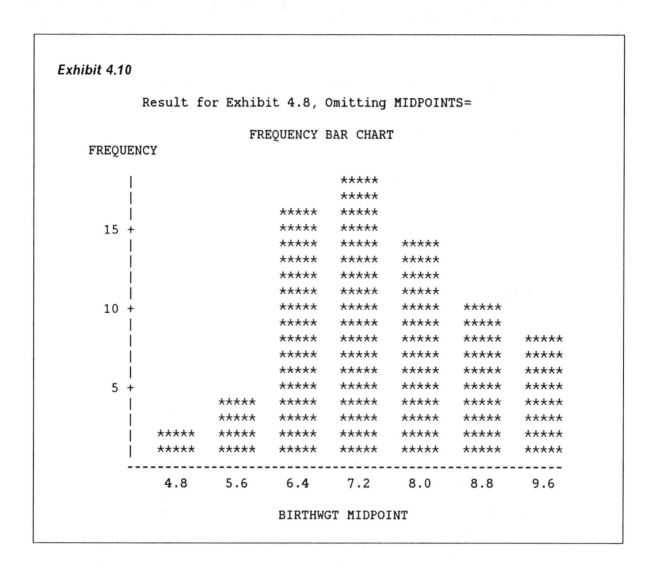

Exhibit 4.10

```
            Result for Exhibit 4.8, Omitting MIDPOINTS=

                          FREQUENCY BAR CHART
      FREQUENCY

              |                                     *****
              |                                     *****
              |                             *****   *****
         15 + |                             *****   *****
              |                             *****   *****   *****
              |                             *****   *****   *****
              |                             *****   *****   *****
              |                             *****   *****   *****
         10 + |                             *****   *****   *****   *****
              |                             *****   *****   *****   *****
              |                             *****   *****   *****   *****   *****
              |                             *****   *****   *****   *****   *****
              |                             *****   *****   *****   *****   *****
          5 + |                             *****   *****   *****   *****   *****
              |                     *****   *****   *****   *****   *****   *****
              |                     *****   *****   *****   *****   *****   *****
              |             *****   *****   *****   *****   *****   *****   *****
              |             *****   *****   *****   *****   *****   *****   *****
              ----------------------------------------------------------------------
                   4.8      5.6     6.4     7.2     8.0     8.8     9.6

                               BIRTHWGT MIDPOINT
```

PROC PLOT

The PLOT procedure can produce one or more plots on the same or different axes. A plot is specified by choosing two variables in the data set—one for the horizontal axis and the other for the vertical axis. A point is plotted for each observation in the data set by taking the values of the two axis variables for that observation and locating the intersection of imaginary lines drawn perpendicularly from the axes at those values.

Statements for PROC PLOT

The PROC PLOT statement is followed by one or more PLOT statements. The PROC PLOT statement is:

>   PROC PLOT DATA = *SASdataset*;

The PLOT statement has the form:

>   PLOT *requests* | *options*;

where "requests" is a list of requested plots. Each request may have one of the following forms:

>   *vertical**horizontal
>   *vertical**horizontal = '*character*'
>   *vertical**horizontal = *variable*

In each form *vertical* is the variable which is to be plotted on the vertical axis and *horizontal* is the variable which is to be plotted on the horizontal axis.

In the first form (*vertical**horizontal), the points are plotted with the letter "A" unless two or more points coincide in which case the letter "B" is used for two coincident points, the letter "C" for three coincident points, etc. (On a line printer plot, it is not uncommon for several points to plot on top of each other because of limited resolution.)

The second form (*vertical**horizontal = '*character*') requests that all points be plotted with the single character specified in the request.

The third form (*vertical**horizontal = *variable*) requests that each observation be plotted with the first character of the value of *variable* for that observation. If more than one observation plots at the same position, the value of *variable* for the first observation is printed (and a note at the bottom of the plot is printed stating how many such observations are hidden.)

Options on the PLOT statement

Many options are described in the *SAS User's Guide*. Here are five of them.

VAXIS = option: Unless this option is specified, the SAS System chooses the values to mark with ticks on the vertical axis. If you wish to specify the values, follow VAXIS= with a list of values (in ascending or descending order). For example,

```
VAXIS = 10 20 30 40
```

produces tick marks at 10, 20, 30, and 40 on the vertical axis. It is possible to use the following notation to specify these values:

```
VAXIS = 10 TO 40 BY 10
```

HAXIS= *option*: The ticks on the horizontal axis are specified in a similar way (if you don't want to use the default). For example,

        HAXIS = 5 TO 15

requests tick marks at values 5, 6, . . ., 15. Note that the BY value is 1, by default.

VREF= *option*: A horizontal reference line is drawn for each value following VREF=. For example,

        VREF = 25

draws one horizontal reference line across the plot at a vertical axis value of 25. Note that it is VREF= since it is vertical values which are specified (for horizontal lines).

HREF= *option*: Vertical reference lines are specified in a similar way. For example,

        HREF = 6 TO 14 BY 2

requests vertical reference lines at horizontal axis values of 6, 8, 10, 12, and 14.

OVERLAY option: Usually, each request is plotted on a separate chart. If you want the requests to plot on the same chart, specify the OVERLAY option. (See an example below.) Note that requests specified on separate PLOT statements are always plotted on separate charts. The OVERLAY option on a PLOT statement applies only to requests on that statement.

Examples

Example 1

The following statements produce a straightforward plot of BIRTHLGH against BIRTHWGT. See Exhibit 4.11. Note the use of the letters "B" and "C" to indicate coincident points.

        PROC PLOT DATA=REPORT;
          TITLE 'Plot of Birth Length and Weight';
          PLOT BIRTHLGH*BIRTHWGT;

Exhibit 4.11

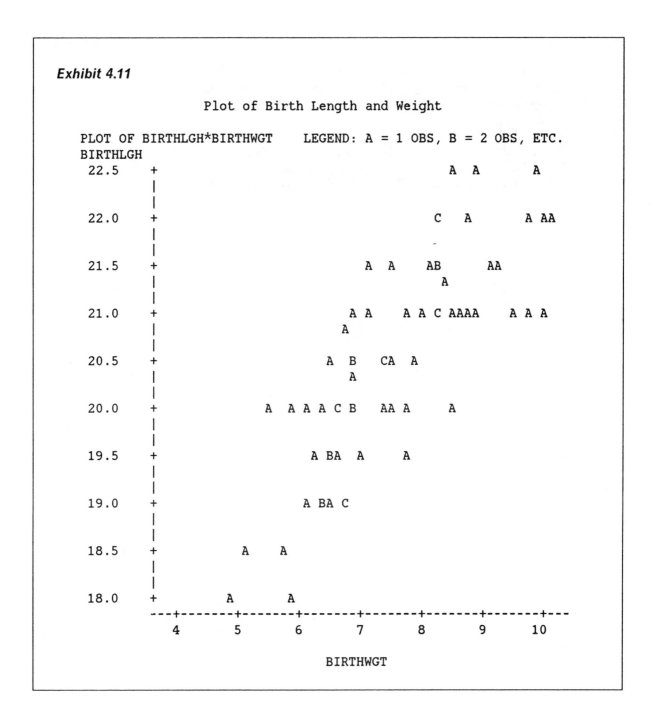

```
                      Plot of Birth Length and Weight

    PLOT OF BIRTHLGH*BIRTHWGT     LEGEND: A = 1 OBS, B = 2 OBS, ETC.
    BIRTHLGH
      22.5   +                                       A  A         A
             |
             |
      22.0   +                                     C   A      A AA
             |
             |                                          -
      21.5   +                           A  A    AB      AA
             |                                       A
             |
      21.0   +                        A A    A A C AAAA    A A A
             |                       A
             |
      20.5   +                    A  B   CA  A
             |                        A
             |
      20.0   +             A  A A A C B  AA A     A
             |
             |
      19.5   +                 A BA  A      A
             |
             |
      19.0   +               A BA C
             |
             |
      18.5   +         A    A
             |
             |
      18.0   +      A       A
             ---+-------+-------+-------+-------+-------+-------+---
                4       5       6       7       8       9      10

                              BIRTHWGT
```

Example 2

The next example is the same plot but with two reference axes drawn and with the code (1 for male and 2 for female) identifying each plotted point. See Exhibit 4.12. Note that there are 15 hidden observations.

```
PROC PLOT DATA=REPORT;
   TITLE 'Plot of Birth Length and Weight, Showing Sex';
   TITLE2 '              1=male, 2=female';
   PLOT BIRTHLGH*BIRTHWGT=SEX / VREF=20 HREF=7;
```

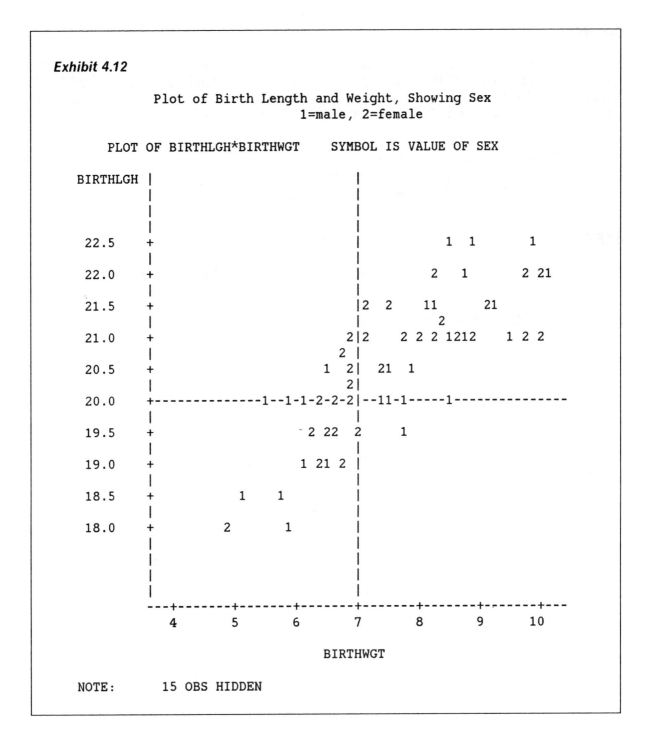

Exhibit 4.12

```
                    Plot of Birth Length and Weight, Showing Sex
                              1=male, 2=female

              PLOT OF BIRTHLGH*BIRTHWGT      SYMBOL IS VALUE OF SEX

       BIRTHLGH |                             |
                |                             |
                |                             |
                |                             |
         22.5   +                             |         1   1          1
                |                             |
         22.0   +                             |      2     1        2  21
                |                             |
         21.5   +                             |2   2     11      21
                |                             |              2
         21.0   +                            2|2      2 2 2 1212    1 2 2
                |                          2  |
         20.5   +                     1    2|   21   1
                |                          2|
         20.0   +--------------1--1-1-2-2-2|--11-1-----1--------------
                |                          |
         19.5   +                    · 2 22  2      1
                |                          |
         19.0   +                    1 21 2 |
                |                          |
         18.5   +           1    1         |
                |                          |
         18.0   +        2          1      |
                |                          |
                |                          |
                |                          |
                |                          |
                ---+-------+-------+-------+-------+-------+-------+---
                   4       5       6       7       8       9      10

                                        BIRTHWGT

       NOTE:    15 OBS HIDDEN
```

Example 3

The final example is actually a nonsensical plot chosen just to illustrate the OVERLAY option. Two plots (one of BIRTHLGH against BIRTHWGT and the other of TESTHGT against TESTWGT) are plotted together. You will see the points from one plot clustered together and the points from the other plot clustered together. See Exhibit 4.13.

```
PROC PLOT DATA=REPORT;
   TITLE 'Overlaid Plots';
   PLOT BIRTHLGH*BIRTHWGT=SEX
        TESTHGT*TESTWGT=SEX / OVERLAY;
```

EXERCISES

1. Explain why there are 15 hidden observations in Exhibit 4.12 by comparing it with Exhibit 4.11.

2. Why is Exhibit 4.13 described as "nonsensical"?

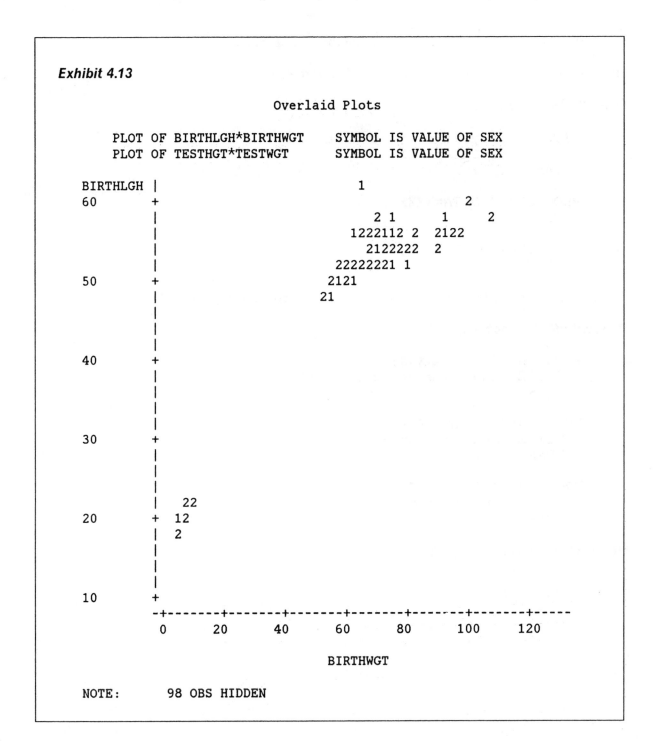

Exhibit 4.13

```
                         Overlaid Plots

         PLOT OF BIRTHLGH*BIRTHWGT    SYMBOL IS VALUE OF SEX
         PLOT OF TESTHGT*TESTWGT      SYMBOL IS VALUE OF SEX


   BIRTHLGH |                              1
   60       +                                        2
            |                         2 1       1      2
            |                       1222112 2  2122
            |                         2122222  2
            |                       22222221 1
   50       +                       2121
            |                       21
            |
            |
            |
   40       +
            |
            |
            |
            |
   30       +
            |
            |
            |
            |     22
   20       +  12
            |  2
            |
            |
            |
   10       +
          --+-------+-------+-------+-------+-------+-------+-----
            0      20      40      60      80     100     120

                              BIRTHWGT

   NOTE:      98 OBS HIDDEN
```

SAS *Tip 6* Using the TITLE Statement

Here are several examples of the use of TITLE statements.

One title for several steps

```
TITLE 'Analysis of test data'
PROC PRINT DATA=XXXX;
  VAR . . .;

PROC CHART DATA=XXXX;
  VBAR . . .;

PROC PLOT DATA=XXXX;
  PLOT . . .;
```

The title "Analysis of test data" will head the output from all three procedures.

Different title for each step

```
PROC CHART DATA=XXXX;
  TITLE 'Analysis of data XXXX'
  VBAR . . .;

PROC CHART DATA=YYYY;
  TITLE 'Analysis of data YYYY'
  VBAR . . .;

PROC CHART DATA=ZZZZ;
  TITLE 'Analysis of data ZZZZ'
  VBAR . . .;
```

Here each analysis has a separate title.

Chapter 5

SOME SAS DESCRIPTIVE PROCEDURES

The previous chapter illustrated some reporting procedures, that is procedures that produce simple listings, charts, and plots. The descriptive procedures MEANS and UNIVARIATE in this chapter go somewhat further: they compute basic statistics such as means and standard deviations. The principal difference between the two PROCs is that PROC MEANS prints a single table for all specified variables whereas PROC UNIVARIATE prints one table of statistics for *each* variable. In order to print all the statistics in a single table, the number of statistics which can be computed by PROC MEANS is smaller than the number which can be computed by PROC UNIVARIATE. In fact, PROC UNIVARIATE always prints all the statistics; in PROC MEANS, you have to specify the statistics you want unless you are satisfied with the few which are printed by default.

Since frequencies are also statistics, there is not a sharp distinction between reporting and descriptive procedures. PROC CHART, discussed in the previous chapter, is presented again with new options to compute frequencies for groups and also to compute sums and means. PROC FREQ, introduced in this chapter, produces tables, rather than charts, of frequencies.

PROC MEANS

The Statlab data contain six variables for which statistics can sensibly be computed. Some basic statistics for these variables are shown in Exhibit 5.1, the output from PROC MEANS. As you see, the output is self-explanatory. The value of "N" is the number of observations for that variable. Unless there are missing values this number is the same for all variables.[1] The output was produced from the following DATA and PROC steps:

```
DATA DEMO;
  INFILE STATLAB;
  INPUT FAMILY $ SEX BLOOD BIRTHLGH BIRTHWGT TESTHGT
        TESTWGT LATERAL PEABODY RAVEN MOTHEDUC MOTHSMOK $;

PROC MEANS DATA=DEMO MAXDEC=2;
  VAR BIRTHLGH BIRTHWGT TESTHGT TESTWGT PEABODY RAVEN;
  TITLE 'Statlab Variables Analyzed by PROC MEANS';
```

Statements for PROC MEANS

In its simplest form a PROC MEANS step consists of these statements:

```
PROC MEANS DATA = SASdataset;
  VAR variables;
```

This PROC step prints one table (such as Exhibit 5.1) displaying the default statistics N,

---

[1] See Chapter 6 for information on missing values.

Exhibit 5.1

Statlab Variables Analyzed by PROC MEANS

VARIABLE	N	MEAN	STANDARD DEVIATION	MINIMUM VALUE	MAXIMUM VALUE
BIRTHLGH	72	20.49	1.09	18.00	22.50
BIRTHWGT	72	7.55	1.24	4.90	10.10
TESTHGT	72	53.81	2.45	48.80	61.10
TESTWGT	72	71.18	11.60	52.00	108.00
PEABODY	72	77.53	8.24	60.00	97.00
RAVEN	72	28.63	9.20	10.00	49.00

MEAN, STANDARD DEVIATION, MINIMUM VALUE, and MAXIMUM VALUE for each variable in *SASdataset* specified in the VAR statement.[2] The VAR statement may be omitted—in that case, PROC MEANS will compute the statistics for every numeric variable in the data set. In the Statlab data set these variables include SEX, BLOOD, etc. which are numeric codes rather than variables for which it is sensible to compute statistics, so it is usually best to list explicitly the variables you want processed.

Options on the PROC MEANS statement

Further control of PROC MEANS may be obtained by including options (in addition to DATA=) on the PROC MEANS statement:

    PROC MEANS DATA=*SASdataset* MAXDEC=*n statistics*;

MAXDEC= option: The MAXDEC= option is used to specify the number of decimal places to be printed in the statistics. (If the option is not given you usually get eight decimal places, most of which are not useful.)

Statistics options: PROC MEANS can compute statistics other than the default statistics listed above. Statistics can be requested by including each statistic name in the PROC MEANS statement. Some of the statistics which can be requested are N, NMISS, MEAN, STD, MIN, MAX, RANGE, SUM, VAR, STDERR, SKEWNESS, KURTOSIS. For example, consider the following PROC step:

    PROC MEANS DATA=XXXX MAXDEC=2
                MEAN VAR RANGE SKEWNESS KURTOSIS;
      VAR AGE WEIGHT;

---

[2] In fact the default statistics printed depend on the length of the printed line. Hence it is usually best to specify what statistics you want rather than using the default.

The output from this step would show (for data set XXXX) only the statistics MEAN, VAR, RANGE, SKEWNESS, KURTOSIS, printed to two decimal places. The usual default statistics (N, etc.), except those specifically requested, would not be printed. The output table for this PROC step would have two lines, one for AGE and one for WEIGHT.

PROC UNIVARIATE

One of the variables in the Statlab data is called PEABODY. It measures the intelligence of the child at age 10 years. The frequency distribution of this variable is shown in Exhibit 5.2.[3] A large number of statistics computed for this variable are shown in Exhibit 5.3, the output from PROC UNIVARIATE. The statistics in Exhibit 5.3 may be compared with the distribution in Exhibit 5.2.

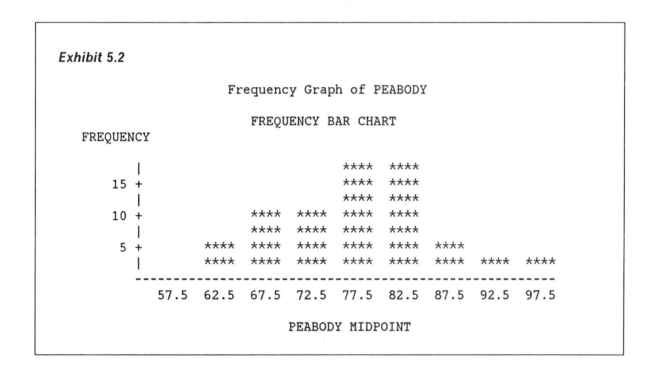

Exhibit 5.2

```
                        Frequency Graph of PEABODY

                         FREQUENCY BAR CHART
     FREQUENCY

          |                                    ****   ****
       15 +                                    ****   ****
          |                                    ****   ****
       10 +                      ****   ****    ****   ****
          |                      ****   ****    ****   ****
        5 +              ****    ****   ****    ****   ****    ****
          |              ****    ****   ****    ****   ****    ****    ****    ****
          -------------------------------------------------------------------
            57.5   62.5   67.5   72.5   77.5   82.5   87.5   92.5   97.5

                          PEABODY MIDPOINT
```

---

[3] The exhibit was produced by these statements:

```
PROC CHART DATA=DEMO;
   VBAR PEABODY / MIDPOINTS=57.5 to 97.5 by 5;
   TITLE 'Frequency Graph of PEABODY';
```

This exhibit illustrates a small difficulty. Note that there is no 57.5 bar. Yet the midpoints were chosen to cover the range of the data. The results from PROC UNIVARIATE in Exhibit 5.3 show that smallest value of PEABODY is 60. This number is exactly half way between the two midpoints 57.5 and 62.5. What does the SAS System do in this case? It turns out that such a value is placed in the higher interval.

Exhibit 5.3

```
                    PEABODY Analyzed by PROC UNIVARIATE

                               UNIVARIATE

        VARIABLE=PEABODY


                                 MOMENTS

                      N              72    SUM WGTS          72
                      MEAN      77.5278    SUM             5582
                      STD DEV   8.24446    VARIANCE      67.971
                      SKEWNESS 0.034133    KURTOSIS   -0.281119
                      USS        437586    CSS          4825.94
                      CV        10.6342    STD MEAN    0.971618
                      T:MEAN=0  79.7924    PROB>|T|      0.0001
                      SGN RANK     1314    PROB>|S|      0.0001
                      NUM ¬= 0       72


                 QUANTILES(DEF=4)                       EXTREMES

        100% MAX     97    99%        97       LOWEST      HIGHEST
         75% Q3      83    95%        93         60           91
         50% MED     78    90%      87.4         62           93
         25% Q1    71.5    10%        66         63           93
          0% MIN     60    5%       64.3         65           96
                          1%         60         65           97

        RANGE        37
        Q3-Q1      11.5
        MODE         78
```

Output from PROC UNIVARIATE

Some of the statistics in Exhibit 5.3 are underlined and are described further here. See the *SAS User's Guide* for information on the other statistics. The output in Exhibit 5.3 is divided into three sections:

Moments: These values include the number of observations (N), the mean (MEAN), and the sum (SUM). The mean is, of course, SUM/N. Next come measures of variability, the standard deviation (STD DEV) and the variance (VARIANCE). Higher-order moments of the distribution are SKEWNESS and KURTOSIS.

Quantiles: The term "quantiles" is a more general term than percentiles; both terms refer to values of the variable which cut off certain proportions of the distribution. For example, the 80% quantile would indicate the value of the variable for which 80% of the observations are lower. The ten quantiles shown include the maximum value (100%), the quartiles (75% and 25%), the median (50%), and minimum value (0%), as well as other percentiles at the extremes of the distribution (99% down to 1%). In addition, the RANGE, MODE, and the interquartile range (Q3–Q1) are shown.[4]

Extremes: Under LOWEST and HIGHEST are listed the five smallest and five largest values of the variable. These lists are often useful, particularly for spotting extreme scores which may have been entered incorrectly.

Statements for PROC UNIVARIATE

A PROC UNIVARIATE step is quite simple:

        PROC UNIVARIATE DATA = *SASdataset*;
           VAR *variables*;

As in PROC MEANS, if the VAR statement is omitted, all numeric variables in the data set are analyzed. Exhibit 5.3 was produced by these statements:

```
PROC UNIVARIATE DATA=DEMO;
  VAR PEABODY;
  TITLE 'PEABODY Analyzed by PROC UNIVARIATE';
```

PROC FREQ

Frequency distribution tables are produced by the following statements:

        PROC FREQ DATA = *SASdataset*;
           TABLES *variables*;

where *variables* are the names of one or more variables whose tables are desired.[5] The variables may be numeric or character.

Exhibit 5.4 was produced by the following statements:

```
PROC FREQ DATA=DEMO;
  TABLES MOTHSMOK;
  TITLE 'Frequency Chart of Smoking History of Mother';
```

Compare this table with the same frequency distribution represented as a chart in Exhibit 2.5.

---

[4] The qualification "DEF = 4" following the word "QUANTILES" means that the fourth definition of quantiles is used (by default). There are five different definitions of quantiles which can be specified! See the *SAS User's Guide* for details.

[5] See more general form of the TABLES statement later in this chapter.

Exhibit 5.4

Frequency Chart of Smoking History of Mother

MOTHSMOK	FREQUENCY	PERCENT	CUMULATIVE FREQUENCY	CUMULATIVE PERCENT
N	39	54.2	39	54.2
Q	14	19.4	53	73.6
01	1	1.4	54	75.0
02	1	1.4	55	76.4
04	1	1.4	56	77.8
06	1	1.4	57	79.2
10	3	4.2	60	83.3
12	1	1.4	61	84.7
13	1	1.4	62	86.1
20	7	9.7	69	95.8
30	1	1.4	70	97.2
35	2	2.8	72	100.0

If frequency tables of both MOTHSMOK and SEX had been desired, the TABLES statement would have been

        TABLES MOTHSMOK SEX;

Two tables would be produced, one for MOTHSMOK and one for SEX. Later in this chapter we will see how to produce a *cross-tabulation* of MOTHSMOK and SEX.

SUMS AND MEANS IN PROC CHART

A fundamental distinction in statistics and in using SAS procedures is between calculating counts and calculating sums. Each frequency calculated by PROCs CHART and FREQ is just a *count* of the number of observations having a particular value of a variable[6] or having values of the variable falling in a certain interval.[7] On the other hand, each mean calculated by PROCs MEANS and UNIVARIATE is the ratio of the *sum* of a variable to the number of observations in the data set.[8] The "number of observations" is itself a count, but unlike the counts computed by PROCs CHART and FREQ is not restricted to a particular value (or interval of values) of a variable. This count is shown in the output of PROCs MEANS and UNIVARIATE as "N". In addition, the output shows the sum as "SUM". The importance of the distinction between counts and sums is that PROC CHART can compute sums and

---

[6] See examples in Exhibits 2.5 and 5.4.
[7] See examples in Exhibits 4.8 and 5.2.
[8] Assuming no missing values; see Chapter 6.

means of a variable for a particular value (or interval of values) of *another* variable. Hence two variables and a sum rather than a count (the default) has to be specified.

For example, suppose you wanted to examine how the test height of an individual depends on their blood type. You might want to display for each blood type the mean test height. Hence two variables have to be specified, BLOOD and TESTHGT, and a mean (the sum of TESTHGT for each blood type divided by the count of observations for that blood type) rather than just a count (frequency) must be calculated.

A different example is shown in Exhibit 5.5. Here we would like to see how the birth-weight depends on the mother's education. Hence we display the mean birth-weight for each of the five categories of mother's education. (Compare these means with the overall mean birth-weight of 7.55 shown in Exhibit 5.1.) In this chart, BIRTHWGT is the variable being summed and MOTHEDUC is the variable whose particular values define each bar. The required PROC step for this chart is:

```
PROC CHART DATA=DEMO;
   VBAR MOTHEDUC / DISCRETE SUMVAR=BIRTHWGT TYPE=MEAN;
   TITLE 'Birth-weight Means by Education of Mother';
```

Note that MOTHEDUC is the variable following "VBAR" and is the variable plotted on the horizontal axis of the chart. BIRTHWGT is defined as the "SUMVAR", the variable being summed. In addition, the TYPE of the chart is defined to be "MEAN", since the default is "SUM".

Statements for PROC CHART for sums and means

Means (or sums) may be obtained by the following statements:

```
PROC CHART DATA = SASdataset;
   VBAR variables / options;
```

where *variables* are the names of one (or more) variables plotted on the horizontal axis of each chart. If several variables are given, one chart is computed for each. The options are of two kinds: those that specify the type of chart (TYPE= and SUMVAR=) and those that specify characteristics of the horizontal axis (DISCRETE, MIDPOINTS=, and LEVELS=).

TYPE= option: There are two possibilities:

- TYPE=MEAN a chart of means

- TYPE=SUM a chart of sums (the default when a SUMVAR is defined)

(See Chapter 4 for values of this option used for charts of frequencies.)

Exhibit 5.5

```
              Birth-weight Means by Education of Mother

                           BAR CHART OF MEANS
   BIRTHWGT MEAN

   8 +                                  *****
     |                                  *****      *****      *****
     |                       *****      *****      *****      *****
     |                       *****      *****      *****      *****
   6 +                       *****      *****      *****      *****
     |            *****      *****      *****      *****      *****
     |            *****      *****      *****      *****      *****
     |            *****      *****      *****      *****      *****
   4 +            *****      *****      *****      *****      *****
     |            *****      *****      *****      *****      *****
     |            *****      *****      *****      *****      *****
     |            *****      *****      *****      *****      *****
   2 +            *****      *****      *****      *****      *****
     |            *****      *****      *****      *****      *****
     |            *****      *****      *****      *****      *****
     |            *****      *****      *****      *****      *****
     -------------------------------------------------------------
                  0           1           2           3           4

                                  MOTHEDUC
```

SUMVAR= option: This option is of the form "SUMVAR = variable", where the variable named is the one which will be summed (for either sums or means). This option is mandatory if sums or means are desired.

Options for the horizontal axis: The options here are precisely those already described in Chapter 4. They are the DISCRETE, MIDPOINTS =, and LEVELS = options. For most charts in which a numeric variable forms the horizontal axis one of these options should be used.

STATISTICS FOR GROUPS AND SUBGROUPS

The analysis just shown could be described as a computation of the means of BIRTHWGT for each education *group* or *subgroup*.   The terms "group" and "subgroup" were not used above since the SAS documentation of PROC CHART uses these terms for a special purpose, which we will describe below.   In fact, the concept of making calculations for groups or subgroups is very general and such calculations can be carried out in the SAS System in many ways.[9]   In this section we show, first, how to calculate frequencies in PROC FREQ for subgroups defined by a cross classification of two or more variables and, second, how to do similar calculations of both sums and counts in PROC CHART.

Two- and multi-way tables in PROC FREQ

Suppose we want to know for each category of mother's education how many children there are of each sex.   That is we want the frequency (count) of observations in each of the education categories subdivided by the sex of the child.   The resulting table may be called a *cross classification* or a *cross tabulation* and is shown in Exhibit 5.6.   The statements needed to produce this table are:

```
PROC FREQ DATA=DEMO;
   TABLES SEX*MOTHEDUC;
   TITLE 'Two-way Frequency Table of SEX by MOTHEDUC';
```

Note the asterisk (*) between the two variables SEX and MOTHEDUC to indicate that subgroups of the two variables in a "two-way" table are desired rather than separate "one-way" tables which would be obtained if the statement

```
TABLES SEX MOTHEDUC;
```

had been used.   Multi-way tables can be specified by joining more variables with asterisks. (However, such tables may produce large amounts of output.)

In general, the following statements are used with PROC FREQ:

```
PROC FREQ DATA = SASdataset;
   TABLES requests / options;
```

where *requests* is a list of single variables (for one-way tables as described earlier in this chapter) or variables joined by asterisks (for two- and multi-way tables).   For example, consider the following statement:

```
TABLES A B*C D E C*E;
```

This statement would produce five tables: a one-way table of A, a two-way table of B and C, one-way tables of D and E, and a two-way table of C and E.   The order of the variables joined by an asterisk is significant: the first one forms the rows of the table, the second the columns.

---

[9] See Chapter 12 for the use of formats to define subgroups of a variable and Chapter 14 for the use of sorted BY-groups.

```
Exhibit 5.6

                  Two-way Frequency Table of SEX by MOTHEDUC

                         TABLE OF SEX BY MOTHEDUC

    SEX         MOTHEDUC

    FREQUENCY|
     PERCENT |
     ROW PCT |
     COL PCT |       0|       1|       2|       3|       4|  TOTAL
    ---------+--------+--------+--------+--------+--------+
           1 |      1 |      7 |     11 |     11 |      6 |     36
             |   1.39 |   9.72 |  15.28 |  15.28 |   8.33 |  50.00
             |   2.78 |  19.44 |  30.56 |  30.56 |  16.67 |
             |  50.00 |  63.64 |  42.31 |  61.11 |  40.00 |
    ---------+--------+--------+--------+--------+--------+
           2 |      1 |      4 |     15 |      7 |      9 |     36
             |   1.39 |   5.56 |  20.83 |   9.72 |  12.50 |  50.00
             |   2.78 |  11.11 |  41.67 |  19.44 |  25.00 |
             |  50.00 |  36.36 |  57.69 |  38.89 |  60.00 |
    ---------+--------+--------+--------+--------+--------+
    TOTAL           2       11      26       18      15        72
                 2.78    15.28   36.11   25.00   20.83    100.00
```

Options on the TABLES statement: The options described here delete one or more of the four entries in each cell of the two-way table.[10] The options are as follows.

- NOFREQ deletes cell frequencies

- NOPERCENT deletes cell percentages

- NOROW deletes row percentages

- NOCOL deletes column percentages

For example, consider the following statement:

        TABLES A*B / NOPERCENT NOROW NOCOL;

The two-way table would have one entry (the frequency) in each cell.

---

[10] These options have no effect on one-way tables.

Groups and subgroups in PROC CHART

Let us call the variable following VBAR the *chart variable*. The chart variable defines the basic intervals on the horizontal axis. So far we have considered two types of charts: frequencies of values of the chart variable and sums (or means) of the "SUMVAR" variable for the values of the chart variable. We now show how more detailed charts can be obtained for groups and subgroups defined by one or two other variables.

GROUP= *option*: The GROUP= option produces several charts side-by-side, one for each value of the GROUP= variable (which is assumed to be discrete). For example, to obtain a chart of number of children in each of the education categories subdivided by the sex of the child, we would use these statements (which produce Exhibit 5.7):

```
PROC CHART DATA=DEMO;
  VBAR MOTHEDUC / DISCRETE GROUP=SEX;
  TITLE 'Frequency Chart of MOTHEDUC Grouped by SEX';
```

(The option DISCRETE is required for MOTHEDUC, as usual.) Note that Exhibit 5.7 (a chart) shows the same counts as Exhibit 5.6 (a table).

SUBGROUP= *option*: The SUBGROUP= option divides each bar by values of the SUBGROUP= variable rather than producing side-by-side charts. The first character of each value of the variable is used to fill in the bar. For example, Exhibit 5.8 was produced by these statements:

```
PROC CHART DATA=DEMO;
  VBAR MOTHEDUC / DISCRETE SUBGROUP=SEX;
  TITLE 'Chart of MOTHEDUC with Bars Subdivided by SEX';
```

Again, this chart provides the same frequencies as the previous table. (Both the GROUP= and SUBGROUP= options can be used, but this is not illustrated here.)

Groups with means: We now go one step further and chart the means of another variable, BIRTHWGT, for each of the education-sex categories. The required statements are:

```
PROC CHART DATA=DEMO;
  VBAR MOTHEDUC / DISCRETE SUMVAR=BIRTHWGT
    GROUP=SEX TYPE=MEAN;
  TITLE 'Graph of Birth-weight Means by MOTHEDUC and SEX';
```

which produced Exhibit 5.9. Compare Exhibits 5.6, 5.7, 5.8, and 5.9; all give statistics for the cross-classification of SEX and MOTHEDUC: the first three give frequencies and the last gives means (of another variable) for each of the combinations of a value of SEX and a value of MOTHEDUC.

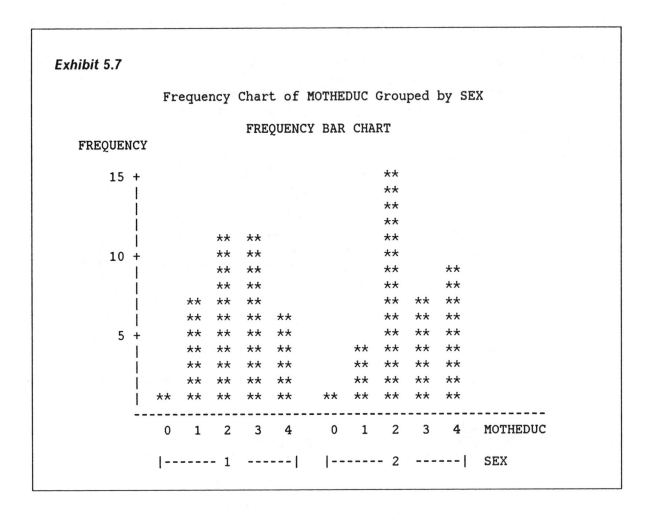

Exhibit 5.7

```
                  Frequency Chart of MOTHEDUC Grouped by SEX

                              FREQUENCY BAR CHART
        FREQUENCY

          15 +                                      **
             |                                      **
             |                                      **
             |                                      **
             |             **   **                  **
          10 +             **   **                  **
             |             **   **                  **        **
             |             **   **                  **        **
             |        **   **   **                  **   **   **
             |        **   **   **   **             **   **   **
           5 +        **   **   **   **             **   **   **
             |        **   **   **   **             **   **   **
             |        **   **   **   **        **   **   **   **
             |        **   **   **   **        **   **   **   **
             |   **   **   **   **   **   **   **   **   **   **
             ---------------------------------------------------------
                 0    1    2    3    4    0    1    2    3    4   MOTHEDUC

                 |------- 1  ------|   |------- 2  ------|   SEX
```

Complete options for the VBAR statement: We summarize the preceding discussion by showing all the options we have discussed. The vertical bar between options denotes "or"; one or the other or both options may be used. For full details of the syntactic conventions used in this book see Appendix A.

VBAR *variables* | *options*;
    options: TYPE = *type* | SUMVAR = *variable* |
        GROUP = *variable* | SUBGROUP = *variable* |
        DISCRETE | MIDPOINTS = *values* | LEVELS = *n*
    type: FREQ | PERCENT | CFREQ | CPERCENT | MEAN | SUM

Exhibit 5.8

Chart of MOTHEDUC with Bars Subdivided by SEX

FREQUENCY BAR CHART

FREQUENCY

```
        |                              22222
        |                              22222
        |                              22222
    20  +                              22222        22222
        |                              22222        22222
        |                              22222        22222        22222
        |                              22222        22222        22222
        |               22222          11111        11111        22222
    10  +               22222          11111        11111        22222
        |               11111          11111        11111        22222
        |               11111          11111        11111        11111
        |   22222       11111          11111        11111        11111
        |   11111       11111          11111        11111        11111
        ------------------------------------------------------------------
            0           1              2            3            4
```

MOTHEDUC

SYMBOL SEX   SYMBOL SEX

1   1   2   2

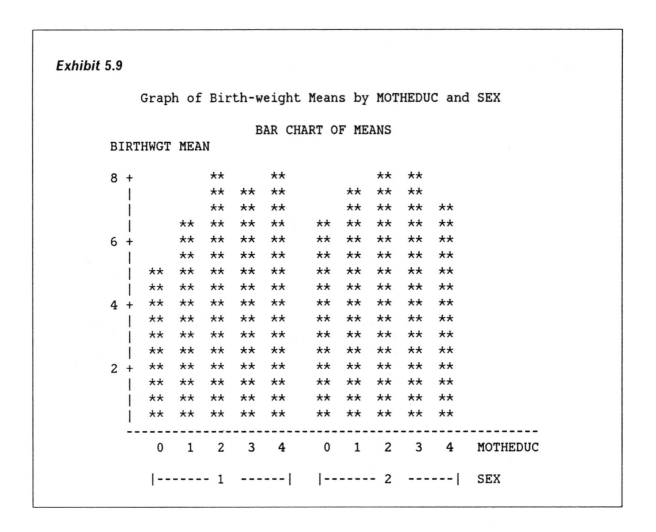

Exhibit 5.9

Graph of Birth-weight Means by MOTHEDUC and SEX

BAR CHART OF MEANS

```
BIRTHWGT MEAN

 8 +           **        **              **  **
   |           **  **  **            **  **  **
   |           **  **  **            **  **  **  **
   |       **  **  **  **        **  **  **  **  **
 6 +       **  **  **  **        **  **  **  **  **
   |       **  **  **  **        **  **  **  **  **
   |   **  **  **  **  **        **  **  **  **  **
   |   **  **  **  **  **        **  **  **  **  **
 4 +   **  **  **  **  **        **  **  **  **  **
   |   **  **  **  **  **        **  **  **  **  **
   |   **  **  **  **  **        **  **  **  **  **
   |   **  **  **  **  **        **  **  **  **  **
 2 +   **  **  **  **  **        **  **  **  **  **
   |   **  **  **  **  **        **  **  **  **  **
   |   **  **  **  **  **        **  **  **  **  **
   |   **  **  **  **  **        **  **  **  **  **
   ---------------------------------------------------------
        0   1   2   3   4        0   1   2   3   4    MOTHEDUC

     |------- 1  ------|    |------- 2  ------|   SEX
```

EXERCISES

1. Note that options on the PROC MEANS statement illustrated in this chapter are *not* preceded by a stroke, "/", whereas options on such statements as the VBAR statement associated with PROC CHART (as illustrated in Chapter 4) *are* preceded by a stroke. Obviously, it is easier not to have to worry about a stroke. Why did the designers of the SAS System have to use a stroke on the VBAR statement but not on PROC statements?

Part 2
THE DATA STEP

In this part we greatly expand on the brief discussion of the DATA step in Part 1. We show that a DATA step can include many of the statements of conventional programming languages, such as assignment, conditional, and looping statements. We describe additional features of the INPUT statement and also show how input can be obtained from a SAS data set instead of from an external file. We also show variations in the output from a DATA step: there can be more than one data set created, the observations on the output data set can be restricted or selected, and output can be to an external file or to the regular print file instead of to a SAS data set.

Chapter 6

THE ASSIGNMENT AND SUM STATEMENTS

In this chapter we describe the assignment and sum statements. Both statements require what are known as *expressions*. Just as variables can be either numeric or character, expressions can be of either type. Numeric expressions are described in this chapter; character expressions in Chapter 7.

THE ASSIGNMENT STATEMENT

The variable BIRTHWGT on the Statlab data set is the child's birth weight in pounds. Suppose we want the birth weight in kilograms. We can create a new variable, BWGTKG, in the following DATA step:

```
DATA METRIC;
   INFILE STATLAB;
   INPUT BIRTHWGT 16-19;
   BWGTKG = BIRTHWGT/2.2;
```

Since one kilogram equals 2.2 pounds, we convert pounds to kilograms by dividing the number of pounds by 2.2.

The statement which performs this calculation is known as an *assignment statement*. The DATA step executes in the following way. The INPUT statement reads one record from the external file STATLAB and stores[1] in the variable BIRTHWGT the number found in columns 16 to 19. Then the assignment statement is executed. First, the right hand side (BIRTHWGT/2.2) is calculated. (The right hand side is known as an *expression*.) Second, the result is stored in the variable BWGTKG. Third, the variables, BIRTHWGT and BWGTKG, are written on the output data set. Then the cycle repeats until all records in the external file have been read.

In general, an assignment statement has the form:

   variable = *expression*;

The effect of such a statement is that *expression* is computed and the result stored in the *variable*.

---

[1] Note that variable names such as BIRTHWGT and BWGTKG actually represent locations in the computer's primary memory. When we say that a value is stored in a variable we mean that it is stored in the primary memory location represented by that variable name. These memory locations are referred to in the SAS System by the term "program data vector", described further in Chapter 17.

NUMERIC EXPRESSIONS

Expressions can be of two types: a numeric expression has a numeric value; a character expression has a character value. The variable on the left hand side of an assignment statement is usually of the same type as the expression.[2] In this section we consider only numeric expressions. See Chapter 7 for character expressions. (A special case of a numeric expression, known as a logical expression, is discussed in Chapter 8.)

A numeric expression is essentially a representation of a numeric formula. For example, the numeric formula for one of the roots of the quadratic equation $ax^2 + bx + c = 0$ is

$$\frac{-b + \sqrt{b^2 - 4ac}}{2a}$$

This formula is represented in the SAS language by the numeric expression:

```
(-B + SQRT(B**2 - 4*A*C))/(2*A)
```

This expression consists of a number of parts, explained in detail below. The parts are:

Numeric constants: 2, 4

Numeric variables: B, A, C

Arithmetic operators: $-$, $+$, * , / , **

Parenthesized expressions: (–B + SQRT(B**2 – 4*A*C)), (2*A)

Function: SQRT

The SAS System interprets each of these parts and performs the requested computation. Once a value has been obtained for the numeric expression (which appears on the right hand side of an assignment statement) it is stored in the variable (which appears on the left hand side of the assignment statement).

Numeric constants

Numeric constants are numbers like 5, −72, 27.6376, −0.4444, +7777.890, etc. The plus sign is optional.

---

[2] See the *SAS User's Guide* for details of what happens when, for example, a character variable = a numeric expression.

Numeric variables

Numeric variables are variables of numeric type. They represent locations in the primary memory of the computer.

Arithmetic operators

There are seven numeric operators in the SAS language. Four of them are the familiar operators for addition (+), subtraction (−), multiplication (*), and division (/). Note that "*", not "×", is used for multiplication and that the asterisk cannot be omitted (as the multiplication sign often is in formulas). Here is an expression using these four operators:

    -2*LENGTH*WIDTH - HEIGHT + DEPTH/45

You can put spaces around the operators (or not), as you wish.

The fifth operator is "**" which means raising to a power. (No space is allowed between the two asterisks.) For example, N**5 directs the SAS System to compute N^5, and A**B directs the SAS System to compute A^B.

The sixth and seventh operators are known as *prefix* operators. They are "+" and "−" but should not be confused with the plus and minus operators previously discussed (which are usually known as *infix* operators). The prefix minus is, in effect, a "change sign" operator. For example, in the expression given above for one root of the quadratic equation, the part "−B" is not a subtraction but rather directs the SAS System to get the value of B and change its sign. Similarly, the expression "+B" directs the SAS System to get the value of B and then keep its sign. Since the prefix plus has no actual effect it is rarely used but might be used to clarify an expression for humans.

Order of operations and parenthesized expressions

Just as in mathematical formulas, there are rules in the SAS language governing the order in which operations are carried out. For example, in

$$a + b \times c$$

the multiplication is carried out before the addition; the formula is equivalent to

$$a + (b \times c)$$

If, on the other hand,

$$(a + b) \times c$$

is intended, then parentheses must be used. The same rules apply to numeric expressions in the SAS language. Each operator has a certain priority which governs when it is performed; the priority can be overruled by the use of parentheses. If you are unsure of the priorities, you can always be safe by using parentheses; however, an expression with many parentheses is hard to read.

The arithmetic operators fall into three priority groups:

Group I: **, prefix +, prefix −

Group II: *, /

Group III: infix +, infix −

Operations in Group I are performed before operations in Group II which are performed before operations in Group III. Operations in Group II are performed in order from left to right. Similarly, operations in Group III are performed in order from left to right. These two groups include the familiar four operators of multiplication, division, addition, and subtraction. Group I is special—it contains the "**" operator and the two prefix operators. Operations in this group are performed in order from *right to left*. For example,

        A** −B

is computed as if it were parenthesized as

        A** (−B)

and

        A**B**C

is computed as if it were parenthesized as

        A**(B**C)

and *not* as

        (A**B)**C

If the latter expression is desired, it must be written as shown with parentheses.

Functions

Functions greatly expand what can be computed in an expression. A function has one or more arguments which specify the values on which the function is computed. A function with one argument is specified by writing its name followed by the argument in parentheses. The argument may be any expression. We have already seen an example of the square root function, SQRT:

        (−B + SQRT(B**2 − 4*A*C))/(2*A)

The expression within the parentheses following SQRT is calculated first; then its value is sent to the square root function (SQRT) which returns the square root. This result is then used in the further computations within the larger expression.

A function with several arguments is specified by writing its name followed by parentheses with the arguments separated by commas within the parentheses. Suppose that X, Y, and Z have the values given by the statements:

```
X = 45.3;
Y = -17;
Z = 222.33;
```

Then the following statement

```
W = MIN(X, Y, Z);
```

assigns W the value -17 since the MIN function returns as value the minimum of its arguments.

There is a vast array of functions supplied with base SAS software. Here are a few. (The variables X, Y, Z defined above are used to illustrate these functions.)

SQRT   square root. For example, SQRT(16) is 4.

ABS   absolute value. For example, ABS(Y) is 17.

MIN   minimum (smallest value), illustrated above.

MAX   maximum (largest value). For example, MAX(X, Y, Z) is 222.33.

MOD   remainder after division of first argument by second. For example, MOD(20, 3) is 2 since 20/3 is 6 with a remainder of 2.

INT   integer part, i.e., truncates decimal part of number. For example, INT(-7.6) is -7 and INT(20/3) is 6 since 20/3 is 6.66666.

FLOOR   largest integer $\leq$ argument. For example, FLOOR(-7.6) is -8 and FLOOR(7.6) is 7.

CEIL   smallest integer $\geq$ argument. For example, CEIL(-7.6) is -7 and CEIL(7.6) is 8.

ROUND   rounds first argument to nearest unit specified by second argument. For example, ROUND(Z, 1) is 222, ROUND(Z, .1) is 222.3, and ROUND(7.6) is 8. (Note that if the second argument is omitted it is assumed to be 1.)

SIN   sine.

COS   cosine.

EXP   exponential, i.e., e ($\approx$ 2.71828) raised to a power.

LOG   natural logarithm (base e).

GAMMA   complete gamma function (used in an example below).

SUM   sum of arguments. For example, SUM(X, Y, Z) is 250.63. The SUM function (and the MEAN function) are particularly useful when one or more arguments are missing. The sum and mean are computed on the non-missing arguments. Missing values are described later in this chapter.

MEAN   mean of arguments. For example, MEAN(X, Y, Z) is 83.54333.

UNIFORM   uniform random numbers (see Chapter 11).

NORMAL   normal random numbers (see Chapter 11).

Further examples

Here are two examples of assignment statements.

Example 1

```
Z = 2.4;
DENSITY = (1.0/SQRT(2*3.1415926536)) * EXP(-Z**2/2);
```

The second assignment statement represents the formula for the density of the normal distribution at a value Z. (The first assignment pre-assigns Z to have the value 2.4.) Here is the formula in conventional mathematical notation:

$$Density = \frac{1.0}{\sqrt{2\pi}} e^{\frac{-z^2}{2}}$$

where $\pi = 3.1415926536$.

Example 2

```
T = 1.7;
F = 1;
DENSITY = GAMMA((F+1)/2)
          / (SQRT(F*3.1415926536)*GAMMA(F/2))
          * (1 + T**2/F)**(-(F+1)/2);
```

Here the lengthy assignment statement represents the formula for the density of a *t*-distribution with f degrees of freedom. The mathematical formula is

$$Density = \frac{\Gamma\left(\frac{f+1}{2}\right)}{\sqrt{f\pi}\,\Gamma\left(\frac{f}{2}\right)}\left(1 + \frac{t^2}{f}\right)^{-\frac{f+1}{2}}$$

where $\Gamma(n)$ is the Gamma function with argument n. (You don't need to know what the Gamma function is to be able to relate the formula to the assignment statement.)

MISSING VALUES

It's impossible to write SAS programs of any length without making errors. Errors can be divided into two types: syntax errors and execution errors. Syntax errors (failures to obey the rules of the language) produce a suitable error message on the SAS log. These errors are considered fatal and processing of the step in error, and all succeeding steps, is discontinued.

On the other hand, most execution errors are not fatal and simply produce a note on the SAS log. For example, suppose in the assignment statement for the density of a t-distribution that you type "G" instead of "F" in one place. When the SAS System attempts to compute this expression it would require the value of G. This variable has no value since it has not been input and has not had an assignment to it. The SAS System recognizes this situation by assigning such variables a special value called a *missing value*. The missing value for a numeric variable is the period ".". When an attempt is made to compute an expression which includes a missing value, the SAS System sets the value of the expression itself to missing. Since the assignment statement assigns the value of the expression to the variable on the left hand side of the statement, that variable will receive a missing value.

Similarly, if you try to divide by zero or to take the square root of a negative number you will get a note on the SAS log and the result of the division or taking the square root will be set to missing.

The missing value for a character variable is blank. Character expressions are discussed in Chapter 7.

Variables which have missing values may still be PROC PRINTed. The observations which have missing values simply show "." for numeric variables and blank for character variables. Furthermore, missing values are not necessarily a sign of error. It is possible that some data read from an external file are missing and the special missing value indication is a convenient way for the SAS System to note these missing data.

THE SUM STATEMENT

One of the unique features of the DATA step is the automatic cycling which takes place over input observations. However, this implicit loop does have a few associated complexities. Some calculations which are easy to do in most programming languages require a special statement in the SAS language.

Suppose you want to add the values of a variable X over all observations.[3] Here is an *incorrect* attempt to do this:

```
DATA WRONG;                    /* Incorrect! */
  TOTAL = 0;
  INFILE XDATA;
  INPUT X;
  TOTAL = TOTAL + X;

PROC PRINT DATA=WRONG;
  VAR X TOTAL;
```

The DATA step, although syntactically correct, does not achieve the desired result since *all* statements in the step are cycled for each observation. This means that TOTAL is reset to zero on each cycle and the TOTAL = TOTAL + X statement simply sets TOTAL = 0 + X on each cycle. The values of X and TOTAL are the same for each observation!

You might think the solution is to delete the TOTAL = 0 statement at the beginning of the DATA step. But this won't work either, because the SAS System sets all variables to the special missing value before each cycle of the DATA step (see discussion of missing values earlier in this chapter). When the TOTAL = TOTAL + X statement is executed, the value of TOTAL on the right hand side is missing which cannot be added to X, so the SAS System generates a message on the SAS log and sets the value of the variable on the left hand side (also TOTAL) to missing.

A special statement is needed to produce the desired result in the SAS System. This statement is called the *sum statement* and it has two functions: it sets the variable in the statement to zero at the beginning of the DATA step (but only once, not on every cycle of the DATA step) and it increments the variable by a specified expression on every cycle of the DATA step. Here is the correct SAS job to sum the values of X:

---

[3] Distinguish this task from the calculation of, say, the sum of X, Y, Z, for *each* observation as in this DATA step:

```
DATA SUMS;
  INFILE XYZDATA;
  INPUT X Y Z;
  SUM = X + Y + Z;

PROC PRINT DATA=SUMS;
  VAR X Y Z SUM;
```

In the example of this footnote there is one sum for each observation. But in the main text we want to sum the values of X for all observations into a single total. There is just one sum for the whole data set.

```
DATA SUM;                /* Correct */
  INFILE XDATA;
  INPUT X;
  TOTAL + X;

PROC PRINT DATA=SUM;
  VAR X TOTAL;
```

The general form of the sum statement is:

variable + expression;

The variable in the sum statement is called an *accumulator* variable. The accumulator variable is set to zero when the DATA step begins. Then on each cycle of the DATA step the accumulator variable is incremented by the value of the expression. In the example, TOTAL is first set to zero and then it is incremented by X on each cycle. The output from PROC PRINT would show this incrementing; for each observation, TOTAL would be the partial sum of all the Xs up to and including that observation. The value of TOTAL for the last observation would be the required sum of all the Xs. (We show later in Chapter 10 how to print just the final sum and not the partial sums.)

Note that the sum statement does not have an equals sign. The sum statement is recognized by its plus sign. A minus sign cannot be used. If you wish to sum the negatives of X, you cannot write

```
TOTAL - X;
```

You must write

```
TOTAL + (-X);
```

Chapter 7

CHARACTER VARIABLES AND THE LENGTH STATEMENT

Recall that variables can be either numeric or character. A variable can be specified as character by placing a "$" after the variable's name in the INPUT statement. In this chapter we describe an alternative way, the LENGTH statement, to specify that a variable is character. The LENGTH statement, as its name implies, is also used to specify the length of a variable. We also describe character expressions and their use in assignment statements.

THE LENGTH STATEMENT

The LENGTH statement is used for two purposes: to specify the type of a variable (numeric or character) and to specify the length of the variable. The default length is 8 bytes. Only infrequently is the length of *numeric* variables changed from the default; see Chapter 16 for details. Here we concentrate on changing the length of *character* variables.

The length of a character variable must be at least as long as the longest *value* which is to be stored in that variable. It is often wise to explicitly declare the length of a character variable in a LENGTH statement before the variable is input or referred to. In this section we give several examples of the difficulties which arise when the LENGTH statement is not used and how these difficulties are overcome by its use.

The form of the LENGTH statement is:

    LENGTH variables [$] length . . .;

where ". . ." indicates that the triplet "variables [$] length" may be repeated. Each variable is given a length and declared to be of character type by the "$". The square brackets indicate that the bracketed item "$" is optional.[1] If "$" is used, the preceding variables are character; if "$" is omitted, the variables are numeric.

Column input

Consider a program which reads two variables, a word and a frequency. Suppose the words can be up to 15 characters long. A straightforward way to create the input external file would be to place the word in columns 1 to 15 and the frequency in, say, columns 16 to 20. Then the lines could be read by the following INPUT statement:

    INPUT WORD $ 1-15 FREQ 16-20;

This INPUT statement declares that WORD is a character variable of length 15 and that FREQ is a numeric variable.

---

[1] Appendix A describes all the the syntactic conventions used in this book.

List input

Now suppose we don't want to use fixed fields in the above example. It is sufficient to follow each word by a blank and then the frequency. For this purpose we use list input:

```
INPUT WORD $ FREQ;
```

List input will sometimes be satisfactory. However, there are several difficulties in this example. The length of WORD defaults to 8 since it is not specified by column input. Hence words longer than 8 characters will be truncated to 8 characters; the frequencies will nevertheless be read correctly. We can use the LENGTH statement to overcome this difficulty:

```
LENGTH WORD $ 15;
INPUT WORD FREQ;
```

Now WORD is declared to be of character type and of length 15 before the INPUT statement. Hence words up to length 15 will be correctly stored in WORD. Note that the "$" must be included in the LENGTH statement or else WORD will be declared as of numeric type. A "$" could still be used in the INPUT statement, but is not necessary since the SAS System knows that WORD is of character type.

List input and the ampersand modifier

Our example still has a difficulty if the "words" have blanks in them. Suppose one of the words is "New York". This word will not be read correctly by the above INPUT statement since the reading of the first variable, WORD, will discontinue at the first blank (resulting in "New" being stored in WORD), and, worse, will lead to an error since the SAS System will next attempt to read "York" as FREQ (a numeric variable).

The SAS language provides a solution: the ampersand modifier. If a variable in an INPUT statement is followed by "&", then reading will continue until two consecutive blanks are read. In other words, if you want to read character values containing single blanks, follow each value by two (or more blanks) and use the ampersand modifier in the INPUT statement. The required statements are now:

```
LENGTH WORD $ 15;
INPUT WORD & FREQ;
```

A final caution. It might be thought that the ampersand modifier solves the problem of character variables longer than the default 8 characters. It does not. You cannot omit the LENGTH statement in the above example. If you write:

```
INPUT WORD $ & FREQ;
```

words longer than 8 characters will still be truncated (although embedded single blanks will be read correctly).

Assignment statement

We now discuss how the length of a character variable may be specified in an assignment statement. The assignment statement itself is discussed more fully in the next main section below and the IF-THEN statement (also used in the examples) in Chapter 8.

Consider the following example:

```
DATA EXAMPLE;
   INFILE STATLAB;
   INPUT FAMILY $ SEX;
   IF SEX = 1 THEN SEXNAME = 'Male';
     ELSE SEXNAME = 'Female';
```

This program will not execute correctly since the character variable SEXNAME will have length 4 and its value for females will be truncated to "Fema". The reasons are as follows. First, the SAS System determines that SEXNAME is a character variable since it is assigned a character value in the statement

```
SEXNAME = 'Male';
```

Second, from the same statement the SAS System determines that SEXNAME has length 4 since the value has length 4. Note that these determinations are made from SEXNAME = 'Male' because that statement is the physically first reference to SEXNAME in the program. Even if the first observation is female and hence the ELSE branch is executed first, the length of SEXNAME is 4.

The solution is to use a LENGTH statement to define the length of the character variable as 6:

```
DATA EXAMPLE;
   LENGTH SEXNAME $ 6;
   INFILE STATLAB;
   INPUT FAMILY $ SEX;
   IF SEX = 1 THEN SEXNAME = 'Male';
     ELSE SEXNAME = 'Female';
```

Note that the "$" is necessary in the LENGTH statement or else the SAS System will attempt in the assignment statements to convert a character value to numeric, resulting in an error.

THE ASSIGNMENT STATEMENT AND CHARACTER EXPRESSIONS

The assignment statement can assign the value of a character expression to a character variable. Suppose an external file NAMES has two fields in each line, representing first and last names. We want to create a new variable, FULLNAME, which is the last name followed by a comma and a space, followed by the first name. For example, if the two names are "Joan" and "Roberts", we want FULLNAME to be "Roberts, Joan". A SAS program to create FULLNAME is:

```
DATA NEWNAMES;
   LENGTH FIRSTN $ 20 LASTN $ 20 FULLNAME $ 40;
   INPUT FIRSTN $ LASTN $;
   FULLNAME = TRIM(LASTN) || ', ' || TRIM(FIRSTN);
   LINES;
Joan Roberts
John Allen
Cynthia MacPherson
;

PROC PRINT DATA=NEWNAMES;
   TITLE 'Creating Full Names';
```

The output from this program is shown in Exhibit 7.1.

Exhibit 7.1

```
                    Creating Full Names

      OBS     FIRSTN      LASTN          FULLNAME

       1      Joan        Roberts        Roberts, Joan
       2      John        Allen          Allen, John
       3      Cynthia     MacPherson     MacPherson, Cynthia
```

The DATA step contains an assignment statement storing the value of a character expression in a character variable. The expression (on the right hand side of the equals sign) consists of several parts (just as an arithmetic expression does):

Character constant: ', '

Character variables: LASTN, FIRSTN

Character operator: ||

Character function: TRIM

The SAS System interprets each of these parts and creates the desired character string as the value of the character expression. It then stores the value in the character variable (appearing on the left hand side of the assignment statement).

Character constants

Character constants are strings of characters enclosed in quotes (either single or double). For example:

```
' , '
'Alpha'
"John's book"
'give me "the answer"'
```

Note that quotes themselves can be included in a character constant by enclosing the constant in quotes of the other type.[2]

Character variables

Character variables are variables of character type (as specified by "$" either in an INPUT statement or in a LENGTH statement).

Character operator

There is only one character operator in the SAS language, namely the *concatenation* operator (||). This operator (two consecutive vertical bars) is an infix operator which takes two character values (i.e., character strings) and produces the combined string. Blanks in these strings are not removed. Hence the need for the TRIM function in the above example.

Character functions

Here are some examples:

TRIM   trim (i.e., remove trailing blanks)

LENGTH   computes length of the argument, i.e., number of characters up to the last non-blank character. For example, LENGTH('abc') is 3. Consider the earlier example where LASTN is a character variable of length 20. If the value of LASTN is

```
             'Roberts                    '
```

then LENGTH(LASTN) is 7, not 20 (the number of bytes of storage used by LASTN) since the last non blank is the seventh character.

REPEAT   REPEAT(X,*n*) returns the value of X followed by *n* repetitions of X. For example, REPEAT('Dd',3) is 'DdDdDdDd'.

---

[2] Character constants may be enclosed in double quotes only if the SAS System option DQUOTE is in effect. See SAS Tip 1: *What you need to know about your computer system* in Chapter 1.

INDEX   INDEX(X, Y) searches X, from left to right, for the first occurrence of the string Y; the result is the position in X of the string Y's first character, or zero if the string is not found. For example, INDEX('abcd','bc') is 2.

SUBSTR   SUBSTR(X,p,n) returns the substring of X starting at position p, of length n. If the third argument is omitted, the substring extending from p to the end of X is returned. For example, SUBSTR('abcdef',3,2) returns 'cd'.

Chapter 8

CONDITIONAL STATEMENTS

There are two types of conditional statements in the SAS language: the IF-THEN statement and the subsetting IF statement. The IF-THEN statement is described in this chapter; the subsetting IF statement is described in Chapter 10. Both types of statements require a *logical expression*; these expressions are described in this chapter.

THE IF-THEN STATEMENT

A very common situation in solving problems (and hence in writing programs) is that a condition is tested—if the condition is true, one branch of the program is to be executed; if the condition is false, another branch is to be executed. As in almost all programming languages, the SAS language handles this situation by an IF-THEN statement of the following form:

> IF *condition* THEN *statement*₁;
>   ELSE *statement*₂;

As you see, these are really two statements: an IF-THEN statement and an ELSE statement. These statements are interpreted as follows. If *condition* is true, then *statement*₁ is executed. If *condition* is false, then *statement*₂ is executed. (How the condition is specified is explained below.) For example, the following statements define the character variable SEXNAME on the basis of the value of the numeric variable SEX:

```
DATA EXAMPLE;
  LENGTH SEXNAME $ 6;
  INFILE STATLAB;
  INPUT FAMILY $ SEX;
  IF SEX = 1 THEN SEXNAME = 'Male';
    ELSE SEXNAME = 'Female';
```

This example was given earlier in Chapter 7, where the necessity of the LENGTH statement was explained.

Two variations of the IF-THEN statement are possible. First, if special action is to be taken only when the condition is true, then the ELSE statement may be omitted. When the condition is false, *statement*₁ is skipped and execution resumes with the next statement after the IF-THEN statement.

Second, suppose you don't want just one statement (*statement*₁ or *statement*₂) to be executed depending on the condition. You want a group of statements to be executed—one group if the condition is true and another group if the condition is false. For this purpose you can use a *DO group* as *statement*₁ and/or *statement*₂. A DO group consists of a *simple DO statement* followed by one or more SAS statements followed by an END statement. That is, a DO group is:

```
DO;
   one or more SAS statements
END;
```

The simple DO group is executed once each time the DO statement is reached.[1] Here is a modification of the above DATA step to illustrate simple DO groups:

```
DATA EXAMPLE;
   LENGTH SEXNAME $ 6;
   INFILE STATLAB;
   INPUT FAMILY $ SEX;
   IF SEX = 1
      THEN DO;
         SEXNAME = 'Male';
         COLOUR = 'Blue';
         END;
      ELSE DO;
         SEXNAME = 'Female';
         COLOUR = 'Pink';
         END;
```

Nested IF-THEN statements

The basic IF-THEN statement provides a two-way branch. Frequently more than two branches are required at a decision point in the program. Nested IF-THEN statements can be used for this purpose. Consider the following segment of a DATA step to compute grades:

```
IF SCORE >= 50 THEN GRADE = 'A';
   ELSE IF SCORE >= 40 THEN GRADE = 'B';
   ELSE IF SCORE >= 30 THEN GRADE = 'C';
   ELSE IF SCORE >= 20 THEN GRADE = 'D';
   ELSE SCORE = 'F';
```

How are these statements interpreted? Technically, there is is just one IF statement (with condition "SCORE > = 50") with a THEN-branch (GRADE = 'A') and an ELSE-branch consisting of an IF statement (IF SCORE > = 40 . . . to end of segment). The new IF statement itself has a THEN- and an ELSE-branch, etc. However, this technical way of interpreting the IF statement can be very confusing. It is easier to look at the segment as a series of IF . . . THEN . . . and ELSE IF . . . THEN . . . statements, each of which expresses the condition for a branch and what is to be executed if the condition is true. The final ELSE-branch is optional; if included, the following statement is executed only if all the preceding conditions are false.

Many programs require such nested IF-THEN statements. In some cases the statement following the "THEN" is a DO group. However, in cases such as the example above which perform, in effect, just a recoding of a variable, a much more direct and less error-prone

---

[1] A DO group begun with a simple DO statement (DO;) is not cycled like a DO group begun with an iterative DO statement (e.g., DO I = 1 TO N;)—see Chapter 11.

method is available in the SAS language: the FORMAT statement (Chapter 12).

LOGICAL EXPRESSIONS

It remains to explain what the *condition* in an IF-THEN statement is. Several examples, such as "SEX = 1", have already been used. In general, a *condition* is a *logical expression*. A logical expression has a value which is true or false. The SAS language does not actually have a separate category of logical expressions. Any numeric expression can be used as a logical expression. A value of zero (or missing) is considered "false". A value of one (or any non-zero value) is considered "true". However, it is easiest to use the terminology "true" and "false" when thinking about conditions and logical expressions.

Logical expressions are formed by combining expressions with *comparison operators*. More complex logical expressions are formed by combining simpler logical expressions with *logical operators*.

Comparison operators

Six comparison operators can be used to compare the values of two expressions. If the comparison is true the value of the logical expression is true; if the comparison is not true the value of the logical expression is false. Here are the six comparison operators. In each case there are two alternative forms in which they can be written.

=	or	EQ	equal to
¬ =	or	NE	not equal to²
>	or	GT	greater than
<	or	LT	less than
> =	or	GE	greater than or equal to
< =	or	LE	less than or equal to

For example, the condition AGE LT 30 is true if AGE is less than 30 and false if AGE is 30 or greater.

Logical operators

There are three operators which can be used with logical expressions. Two of them are infix operators combining two logical expressions:

&	or	AND	logical and
|	or	OR	logical or

(Either of the two forms shown on the left may be used.) For example, consider the following expression:

```
(SEX = 1) AND (AGE LT 30)
```

---

² On some computers you must use ^= (or NE) for this comparison operator.

This expression is true for those observations which have both SEX = 1 and AGE < 30. Note that parentheses have been included in the expression to ensure that the inner expressions are evaluated before the "AND". Actually, the comparison operators have higher priority than the logical operators and so would be performed first in any case.

The third logical operator is a prefix operator:

     ¬   or   NOT   logical not[3]

(Either of the two forms shown on the left may be used.) For example:

```
(X >= 55) AND NOT (Y = .)
```

will be true when $X \geq 55$ and the variable Y is not missing (since a missing value for numeric variables is indicated by a period).

---

[3] On some computers you must use ^ (or NOT) for this logical operator.

Chapter 9

SOURCES OF INPUT

So far we have described only one way to read data into a DATA step, namely by an INPUT statement reading in-stream data or an external file. Data may also be read from an existing SAS data set by a SET statement. In this chapter we discuss the SET statement and also discuss a few additional features of the INPUT and INFILE statements.

THE SET STATEMENT

Consider the following example of two DATA steps and one PROC step.

```
DATA TEMP;
   INFILE XYZDATA;
   INPUT X Y Z;

DATA SUMS;
   SET TEMP;
   SUM = X + Y + Z;

PROC PRINT DATA=SUMS;
```

The two DATA steps and their associated external file and data sets can be summarized in the following diagram:

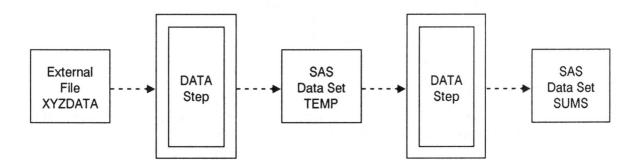

The first DATA step inputs the three variables from an external file and creates the SAS data set TEMP. The second DATA step inputs the data from TEMP (using the SET statement) and then carries out a calculation. The second DATA step creates a new SAS data set SUMS. The PROC PRINT step (not shown in the diagram) processes SUMS and prints the four variables X, Y, Z, and SUM.

In this simple example it is not necessary to have two DATA steps. The same result could have been achieved by:

```
DATA SUMS;
   INFILE XYZDATA;
   INPUT X Y Z;
   SUM = X + Y + Z;

PROC PRINT DATA=SUMS;
```

However, it is very common to write DATA steps which have a SAS data set as their input, particularly if the data set is permanent. The above example consisted only of temporary data sets.[1]

The SET statement has the form:

> SET *SASdataset*;

where *SASdataset* is the data set to be input. On each cycle of the DATA step, the values of the variables for one observation of the input data set are available. The DATA step continues cycling until the observations in the data set are exhausted. This is the implicit loop of the DATA step.

Note that no INPUT statement is used with the SET statement. Note further that the SET statement, like the INPUT statement, instructs the SAS System to cycle over observations and to output all the variables to the output data set at the end of each cycle.

INPUT EXTENSIONS

In this section we allow more flexibility in the way data are read from an external file by an INPUT statement. Chapter 3 described the basic forms of list and column input. The extensions described here are used with these basic forms.

The ampersand modifier (&)

The ampersand modifier is used to input a character value with single embedded blanks in list input. The ampersand modifier was described earlier; see Chapter 7.

The column pointer controls (@n, +n)

Suppose there are some fields on a data line that you do not want to read; that is, you want to skip over them. You can do this in two ways. Usually you would use column input to specify those fields you want to read. Alternatively, you can specify the starting column of a field and then use list input to read the field. You use the column pointer controls "@*n*" and "+*n*" for this purpose. For example, "@20" specifies that reading continues from column 20 on the data line; "+13" specifies that 13 columns are skipped. The *column pointer* is used by the SAS System to keep track of the column at which reading is taking place. The column pointer is automatically changed after each variable on an INPUT statement is read. "@*n*" specifies

---

[1] See the discussion of temporary and permanent data sets in Chapter 3.

an absolute value of the pointer; "+n" specifies a relative value, i.e., a change in the pointer's value.

Consider the following INPUT statement:

```
INPUT X @20 Y Z +15 W;
```

X would be read by list input. Then the pointer is moved to column 20 and Y and Z are read by list input. Then the pointer is moved 15 columns to the right (from where it was left after Z was read) and W is read by list input.

The line pointer controls (#n, /)

Sometimes the data for an observation are on two or more data lines. The line pointer controls are used to specify the lines. "#n" is used to move to line n; "/" is used to advance to the next line. For example,

```
INPUT X Y #2 Z;
```

specifies that X and Y are to be read from the first line and Z from the second, for each observation. Alternatively, this INPUT statement could be written:

```
INPUT X Y / Z;
```

The double trailing at-sign (@@)

It is occasionally useful to have more than one observation on one data line. The double trailing at-sign is used for this purpose. For example,

```
DATA MANY;
  INPUT X Y @@;
  LINES;
2 4 5 7 3 8 5 9
15 18 20 22
  ;
```

Six observations are created by this DATA step: in the first, the values of X and Y are 2 and 4; in the second, the values are 5 and 7, etc.

INFILE EXTENSIONS

Characteristics of the external file are specified on the INFILE statement as options.

The FIRSTOBS= and OBS= options

If you have a lengthy external file, you might want to read only part of this file, particularly for testing purposes. The FIRSTOBS= option specifies the line number of the first data line to be read and the OBS= option specifies the line number of the last line to be read. For example, to read the 51st through 100th lines on the file with *fileref* MYDATA, use the statement:

```
INFILE MYDATA FIRSTOBS=51 OBS=100;
```

DETECTING END OF FILE

There are many situations in which you want the DATA step to take a special action when the end of the external file (or input SAS data set) is reached. This process may be called "detecting end of file", for SAS data sets are also, after all, files. However, the special actions which are to be taken are generally output actions, that is writing on an output data file. The ways to carry out these actions are described in the next chapter, so we defer to that chapter the discussion of the END= option on the INFILE and SET statements.

Chapter 10

OUTPUT FROM THE DATA STEP

In the last chapter we have seen that SAS data sets as well as external files can be input to a DATA step. So far the only output from a DATA step has been a SAS data set. In this chapter we show that a DATA step can also have an external file as output. In addition we show how to have several data sets as output from one DATA step and how to restrict the observations on the output data set.

WRITING ON AN EXTERNAL FILE

In earlier chapters, the term "external file" referred to a data file which is input to a DATA step. More generally, an external file is a file which can be processed by programs other than the SAS System. Not only can the SAS System read such files, but it can output such files. The output data file produced by PROC steps is an external file since it can be printed. To reduce ambiguity, let us now refer to it as the *standard SAS print file*.

A DATA step can write on the standard SAS print file or it can create other external files. In either case the file is defined by a FILE statement and the lines on it are written by a PUT statement. These statements (for writing external files) are parallel to the INFILE and INPUT statements (for reading external files).

The FILE statement

The form of the FILE statement is:

   FILE *fileref*;

where *fileref* is either defined in an operating system statement (just as for an INFILE statement—see Chapter 3) or else is one of the special *fileref*s PRINT or LOG. If the *fileref* is PRINT, all lines produced by PUT statements go to the standard SAS print file. If the *fileref* is LOG, all lines produced by PUT statements go to the SAS log. (By default, if no FILE statement is given, all lines go to the SAS log, so this *fileref* is not usually needed.)

The PUT statement

Variables may be written in *list style* or in *column style*, closely matching list and column input in the INPUT statement. For example, the statement

```
PUT X Y Z 20-25;
```

writes a line with the values of X and Y separated by one blank (list style) and the value of Z in columns 20 to 25 (column style).

Character constants can also be included in the PUT statement:

```
PUT 'The two results are: ' X Y ' for Z = ' Z 20-25;
```

Named output is an alternative way to identify individual variables. If a variable name is followed by an equals sign (=), the variable name itself as well as its value is written. For example,

```
PUT X= Y= Z=;
```

might produce:

```
X=25.3 Y=-1.1 Z=45.323
```

For further examples of PUT statements (and some extensions described in the next section) see Chapter 15. Another way to write the variables is called *formatted style*, described in Chapter 12.

PUT EXTENSIONS

Additional features of the PUT statement include column pointer controls ($@n$, $+n$) and line pointer controls ($#n$, /) just as on the INPUT statement. Two more line pointer controls are also described (_PAGE_ and OVERPRINT).

The column pointer controls ($@$n, $+$n)

The column pointer is moved to the column specified by "$@n$" or is moved by n columns if "$+n$" is used. For example,

```
PUT X @ 20 Y Z +15 W;
```

writes X starting in column 1 (list style), writes Y and Z starting in column 20 (list style), and writes W (also in list style) starting 15 columns to the right of the last column printed for Z.

The line pointer controls (#n, /, _PAGE_, OVERPRINT)

Writing is moved to the line specified by "$#n$" or to the next line if "/" is used. For example,

```
PUT X Y #10 Z;
```

writes X and Y on the next line on the page and writes Z on line 10 (which might be above or below the line on which X and Y are written). More frequently, one uses "/" to specify output on two successive lines:

```
PUT X Y / Z;
```

The pointer control "_PAGE_" is used when the next output is to appear on a new page. For example,

```
PUT X Y;
PUT _PAGE_;
PUT Z;
```

writes X and Y, moves to a new page, and writes Z as the first line on the new page. The three PUT statements can be combined into one statement:

```
PUT X Y _PAGE_ Z;
```

Finally, OVERPRINT writes over the previous line. For example,

```
PUT 'The Results' OVERPRINT '_____';
```

produces an underscored heading.

CREATING MORE THAN ONE OUTPUT DATA SET

More than one data set can be specified on the DATA statement. Unless an OUTPUT statement is used (see below) all observations are written on all the data sets listed in the DATA statement.

More commonly, one would like to create, say, two different data sets. The following DATA step creates two data sets, one of males and the other of females in the Statlab data.

```
DATA MALES FEMALES;
   INFILE STATLAB;
   INPUT FAMILY $ SEX BLOOD BIRTHLGH BIRTHWGT TESTHGT
      TESTWGT LATERAL PEABODY RAVEN MOTHEDUC MOTHSMOK $;
   IF SEX = 1 THEN OUTPUT MALES;
     ELSE OUTPUT FEMALES;
```

The OUTPUT statement

The OUTPUT statement has the form:

OUTPUT [*SASdataset*] . . .;

where zero, one, or more data sets may be named on the statement. Only data sets listed on the DATA statement may be listed on the OUTPUT statement. When the OUTPUT statement is reached during execution of the DATA step, the current observation is written on all the data sets listed on the OUTPUT statement. If none are listed, the current observation is written on all the data sets listed in the DATA statement.

When does output occur?

Introducing the OUTPUT statement alerts us to some complications in the execution of the DATA step. If a DATA step does not have any OUTPUT statement, then the current observation is always output at the end of each cycle of the DATA step unless restricted by a subsetting IF, DELETE, or STOP statement (described later in this chapter). However, if a DATA step has an OUTPUT statement, then no output occurs automatically. Output only occurs (to a SAS data set) when an OUTPUT statement is reached during execution. See Chapter 17 for a detailed explanation of how the DATA step executes.

DETECTING END OF FILE ON INPUT

In Chapter 6 we used the sum statement to accumulate the total of the values of X for all observations. The total was correctly computed but the printing of it by PROC PRINT was unsatisfactory. The output data set contained all the partial sums, one for each of the observations on the input data set. What we really want is an output data set with only one observation, whose value of TOTAL is the grand total.

In order to achieve this result we have to arrange two things: first, we have to suppress writing observations on the output data set while the input file is read and the partial sums are computed and, second, we have to write one observation *after* all the observations have been read. We will use an OUTPUT statement to write the single observation. As described above, whenever an OUTPUT statement is used, the SAS System suppresses any automatic writing of observations on the output data set. The only observations written are those written by the OUTPUT statement. In addition we have to use an option, not previously discussed, which will detect the end of the input observations. The END= option can be used on either an INFILE statement:

    INFILE *fileref* END = *endvariable*;

or on a SET statement:

    SET *SASdataset* END = *endvariable*;

When these statements are used the SAS System creates a new variable *endvariable*. Its value is set to 0 (false) for every observation except the last. When the last observation is read, *endvariable* is set to 1 (true).

Here is how the example in Chapter 6 can be written to produce just one total on the output data set.

```
DATA ONLYSUM;
  INFILE XDATA END=LAST;
  INPUT X;
  TOTAL + X;
  IF LAST THEN OUTPUT;

PROC PRINT DATA=ONLYSUM;
  VAR TOTAL;
```

The IF statement tests the value of LAST on each cycle of the DATA step. For every observation except the last, the value of LAST is 0 (false), the condition of the IF is false, and the THEN clause is not executed. However, on the last observation, LAST is true, the THEN clause is executed, and the single observation is written. Hence the output data set has one observation; there are two variables in that observation: X (for the last input observation) and TOTAL. We actually don't want X, but it does no harm and is not printed because we used the VAR statement with PROC PRINT.[1]

The same principles apply to the use of the END= option on either the INFILE or the SET statement. Since a SAS data set, like an external file, is just a computer file, we say that in either case the END= option is used to detect the end of file.

RESTRICTING THE OBSERVATIONS

The SAS language provides three statements which can prevent observations from being written on the output data set. These statements are the subsetting IF statement, the DELETE statement, and the STOP statement.

The Subsetting IF statement

Suppose you want only males to be written on the output data set and suppose that males are coded 1 in the variable SEX. The following DATA step has the desired result:

```
DATA MALES;
  INFILE RESULTS;
  INPUT SEX X Y Z;
  IF SEX = 1;
```

The expression "SEX = 1" is, of course, a *condition* or a *logical expression*. The condition is either true (when SEX = 1) or false (when SEX ≠ 1, i.e., when SEX = 2). The DATA step is executed as follows: read the values of SEX, X, Y, and Z for the next observation; determine if the value of SEX is "1"—if it is, the condition is true and the observation is written on the output data set; if it is not, the observation is not written. In either case, the DATA step then recycles to read the next observation.

The general form of the subsetting IF statement is:

IF *condition*;

When *condition* is true, the DATA step continues and following statements (if any) are executed. When *condition* is false, the current cycle of the DATA step is terminated.

---

[1] It is possible to prevent X being written on the output data set—see the KEEP statement discussed in Chapter 16. In any case, the *endvariable* LAST is not written on the output data set.

The DELETE statement

When the DELETE statement is executed the current cycle is terminated, no observation is written on the output data set, and the next cycle of the DATA step begins. The DELETE statement is usually used as the THEN clause of an IF-THEN statement:

IF *condition* THEN DELETE;

When *condition* is true, the observation is "deleted" (not written on the output data set) and the next cycle of the DATA step begins. If *condition* is false, the observation is not deleted and the execution of the current cycle of the DATA step continues.

The previous example (to write a data set of only male observations) could have been written:

```
DATA MALES;
   INFILE RESULTS;
   INPUT SEX X Y Z;
   IF SEX = 2 THEN DELETE;
```

The subsetting IF and the DELETE statement can be contrasted in the following way. The subsetting IF statement essentially says:

IF *condition* THEN carry on this cycle

whereas the DELETE statement (in an IF-THEN statement) essentially says:

IF *condition* THEN do not carry on this cycle

An equivalent way to contrast the statements is to note that the subsetting IF statement:

IF *condition*;

can always be replaced by the following statement:

IF NOT *condition* THEN DELETE;

If *condition* is true then NOT *condition* is false, the THEN clause is not executed, and execution of the current cycle continues with the next statement following the IF-THEN statement. However, if *condition* is false then NOT *condition* is true, the THEN clause is executed, the DELETE statement is executed, and the current cycle is terminated.

The STOP statement

The STOP statement discontinues the whole DATA step, not just one cycle as the DELETE statement does. Suppose that you want to create a data set consisting of only the first 40 observations from the input file. This task can be done as follows. There is an "automatic variable" _N_ which is always computed in a DATA step. It is the cycle number, i.e., the number of observations which have so far been processed. The required DATA step would use this automatic variable:

```
DATA FORTY;
   INFILE RESULTS;
   INPUT SEX X Y Z;
   IF _N_ > 40 THEN STOP;
```

Just as the DELETE statement, the STOP statement is usually part of the THEN clause of an IF-THEN statement. The general form is:

IF *condition* THEN STOP;

In the above example the condition is "_N_ > 40", which is false for the first 40 observations, so each of those is written on the output data set. However, on the 41st observation, _N_ = 41, so that the condition is true and the execution of the DATA step is terminated, leaving an output data set with 40 observations. Of course, if there were fewer than 40 data lines in the input file then all the observations would be written on the output data set.

Chapter 11

EXPLICIT LOOPING

The DATA step has a built-in mechanism for cycling or looping over all observations in the input data set or external file. In contrast to this implicit looping it is possible to create loops oneself. These explicit loops are described in this chapter.

DO LOOPS

Suppose we want to create a conversion table which shows the kilograms for every value of pounds from 0.0 to 20.0 in steps of 0.1. One, impractical, way to do this is as follows:

```
DATA LONG;
   INPUT POUNDS;
   KILOGRAM = POUNDS/2.2;
   LINES;
0.0
0.1
0.2
 . . .
19.9
20.0
;

PROC PRINT DATA=LONG;
   TITLE 'Conversion of pounds to kilograms';
   ID POUNDS;
   VAR KILOGRAM;
```

This is impractical since all the pounds from 0.0 to 20.0 would actually have to appear after the LINES statement (most are shown by ". . ." above); a great deal of work would have to be done to generate these data lines.

What we need for this task is a program to generate the values of POUNDS from 0.0 to 20.0. This can be done by a *loop*. Here is a DATA step to do this (the PROC PRINT step would be unchanged except for the data set specified in DATA=).

```
DATA SHORT;
   DO POUNDS = 0.0 TO 20.05 BY 0.1;
      KILOGRAM = POUNDS/2.2;
      OUTPUT;
      END;
```

Note first that there is no INPUT statement in this DATA step (nor LINES or INFILE statements). The values of POUNDS and KILOGRAM are generated in the DATA step itself. The DO loop (beginning with the DO statement and ending with the END statement) creates each pair of values and outputs the pair to the output data set. The DO statement specifies that the value of POUNDS is to be set successively to 0.0, 0.1, etc. up to 20.0 (the reason why the upper limit is specified as 20.05 and not 20.0 will be explained shortly). For each value of POUNDS, all the statements in the loop are executed. In this example there are just two statements in the loop (not counting the END statement). The first is the assignment statement which creates KILOGRAM from the value of POUNDS. The second is the OUTPUT statement. When the OUTPUT statement is executed, the values of all variables are written as one observation on the output data set.

The DO statement has the form:

> DO *indexvariable* = *start* TO *stop* [BY *increment*];

The END statement is simply:

> END;

The statements in a DATA step from the DO statement to the END statement are known as a DO group. In fact the above DO statement is better described as an *iterative DO statement* in contrast to the simple DO statement (Chapter 8).

How is a DO statement executed? First, *indexvariable* is set to the value of *start*. Then the DO group is executed. Then *indexvariable* is increased by the value of *increment* and the DO group is executed again. (The "BY *increment*" part of the DO statement may be omitted, in which case *increment* is 1, by default.) This cycle is repeated until the value of *indexvariable* exceeds *stop*. In other words, the DO group is executed for all values of *indexvariable* $\geq$ *start* and $\leq$ *stop*.

Why, then, in the example above was *stop* = 20.05 instead of 20.0, which is the final desired value of POUNDS?   The difficulty is that numbers, such as 5.1, 5.2, etc., which are not integers, cannot be represented exactly in the computer. When 0.1 (the increment) is added successively to 0.0, the results are not exactly 0.1, 0.2, etc. (However, they still print correctly since PROC PRINT ignores such small discrepancies.) Hence when 20.0 is reached, the result is not exactly 20.0; it might be slightly below 20.0 or slightly above it. If *stop* had been set to 20.0, and the value of *indexvariable* was slightly below 20.0, all is well—the DO group is executed for this value and when *indexvariable* is again incremented, the value is above 20.0 and the loop terminates. However, if the value of *indexvariable* was slightly above 20.0, then the DO group would not be executed for this value so that the last value of POUNDS which would appear in the table would be 19.9. Setting *stop* = 20.05 (or some other number between 20.0 and 20.1) solves this problem. The DO group will then always be executed for a value of *indexvariable* near 20.0.

Example

We now have the tools to generate mathematical distributions. For example, here is a SAS program to compute and plot the normal distribution.[1]

---

[1] The assignment statement in this example was discussed in Chapter 6.

```
DATA NORDIST;
  DO Z = -4 TO 4.05 BY 0.2;
    DENSITY = (1.0/SQRT(2*3.1415926536)) * EXP(-Z**2/2);
    OUTPUT;
    END;

PROC PLOT DATA=NORDIST;
  PLOT DENSITY*Z / HAXIS = -4 TO 4 BY 1;
  TITLE 'Normal Distribution';
```

The DO loop is similar to the one we have just described. The value of Z is cycled from −4 to 4 in steps of 0.2. Note that the value of *stop* in the DO statement is set to 4.05 to ensure that the loop is actually executed for the final value of 4. The OUTPUT statement is essential; otherwise only one observation (for Z = 4) will be written on the output data set. See Chapter 17 for further explanation of the OUTPUT statement. The output from PROC PLOT is shown in Exhibit 11.1.

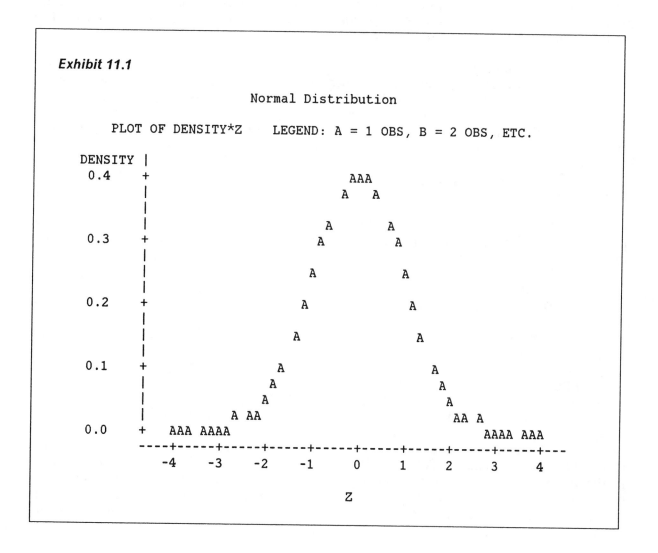

Exhibit 11.1

GENERATING RANDOM NUMBERS

You might think it impossible for a computer to generate random numbers. After all, a computer is a deterministic device. However, it is possible to generate numbers which are not truly random but are called pseudo-random numbers. These pseudo-random numbers have been thoroughly tested and, for most purposes, have the properties of truly random numbers. An explanation of how these numbers are generated and tested is beyond the scope of this book. Suffice it to say that, in the simplest method, an initial number is chosen (called the *seed*). This number is multiplied by a large, fixed number, producing, in general, a number twice as long as the initial number. The number is chopped in half and the right half is the generated pseudo-random number which also becomes the new initial number (i.e., the new seed). For each required random number the process is repeated.

The choice of the initial seed is very important. When random numbers are used extensively in a simulation and when it is important to have control over the generation of the random numbers, the SAS System provides methods for the user to specify the seed. However, this should not be done without careful thought. For most purposes, it is sufficient to have the SAS System use its default method of choosing the seed equal to the time of day. This method is used in all the examples below.

Each sequence of random numbers generated by a computer program comes from a specified probability distribution. The most basic distribution is a uniform distribution between, say, 0 and 1. This means that any real number between 0 and 1 has an equal probability of being generated. The next subsection explains how to generate uniform random numbers. The most frequently used probability distribution is the normal distribution. The second subsection explains how to generate normal random numbers.

Uniform random numbers

Exhibit 11.2 shows the distribution of 100 uniform random numbers, generated to have equal probabilities of any value between 0 and 1. The program which generated this exhibit was the following:

```
DATA UNIFORMA;
  DO I = 1 TO 100;
    Y = UNIFORM(0);
    OUTPUT;
    END;

PROC CHART DATA=UNIFORMA;
  VBAR Y / MIDPOINTS = 0.05 to 0.95 BY 0.1;
  TITLE 'Uniform Random Numbers in Interval (0, 1)';
```

In the DATA step a loop is executed 100 times. The loop contains an assignment statement and an OUTPUT statement. The assignment statement is Y = UNIFORM(0); which assigns to the variable Y the value of the function UNIFORM. UNIFORM is the function which produces random numbers from the uniform distribution (on the interval 0 to 1). The argument of the function is zero; this value of the argument requests the default seed based on

Exhibit 11.2

Uniform Random Numbers in Interval (0, 1)

FREQUENCY BAR CHART

FREQUENCY

```
       |                        ***                                 ***
       |                        ***                                 ***
       |     ***                ***                    ***          ***
       |     ***                *** ***                *** ***      ***
   10 +     ***                *** ***                *** *** ***
       |     ***                *** ***        ***     *** *** ***
       |     ***                *** ***        ***     *** *** ***
       |     ***                *** ***        ***     *** *** ***
       |     *** ***     ***    *** ***        ***     *** *** ***
    5 +     *** *** ***    *** *** *** ***     *** *** *** ***
       |     *** *** ***    *** *** *** ***     *** *** *** ***
       |     *** *** ***    *** *** *** ***     *** *** *** ***
       |     *** *** ***    *** *** *** ***     *** *** *** ***
       |     *** *** ***    *** *** *** ***     *** *** *** ***
       -----------------------------------------------------------
         0.05 0.15 0.25 0.35 0.45 0.55 0.65 0.75 0.85 0.95
```

Y MIDPOINT

the clock time, as discussed above. All the examples of random functions in this chapter will use an argument of zero.

You see in the exhibit that the frequency distribution is not precisely uniform. This is to be expected since the numbers forming the frequency distribution were random. Note the choice of midpoints in PROC CHART. These midpoints ensure that the intervals are 0.0 to 0.1, 0.1 to 0.2, etc. (Why would MIDPOINTS = 0 TO 1 BY 0.1 be unsatisfactory?)

Suppose we want to have random numbers uniform in the interval from 20 to 36, instead of the default interval. In general, numbers, x, which range from 0 to 1 can be converted to numbers, y, which range from a to b by the formula

$$y = (b - a) \times x + a$$

Here is a SAS program to generate 500 numbers uniform in the interval from 20 to 36:

```
DATA UNIFORMB;
  A = 20;
  B = 36;
  DO I = 1 TO 500;
    Y = (B - A)*UNIFORM(0) + A;
    OUTPUT;
    END;

PROC CHART DATA=UNIFORMB;
  VBAR Y / MIDPOINTS = 21 TO 35 BY 2;
  TITLE 'Uniform Random Numbers In interval (20, 36)';
```

The output is shown in Exhibit 11.3.

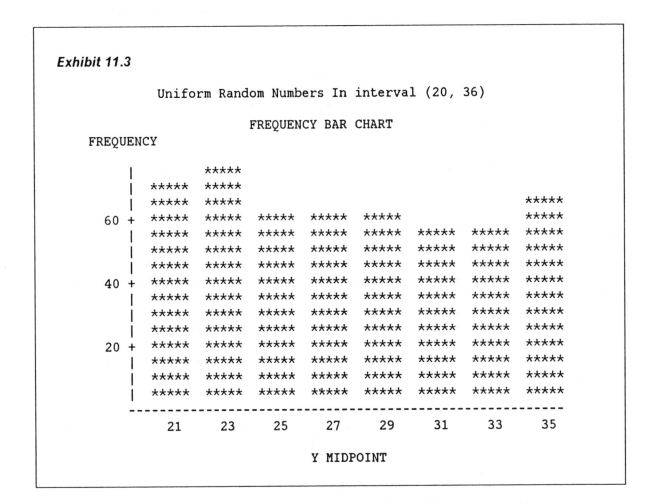

Exhibit 11.3

```
        Uniform Random Numbers In interval (20, 36)

                    FREQUENCY BAR CHART
FREQUENCY

          |            *****
          |      *****  *****
          |      *****  *****                                      *****
      60 +       *****  *****  *****  *****  *****                  *****
          |      *****  *****  *****  *****  *****  *****  *****  *****
          |      *****  *****  *****  *****  *****  *****  *****  *****
          |      *****  *****  *****  *****  *****  *****  *****  *****
      40 +       *****  *****  *****  *****  *****  *****  *****  *****
          |      *****  *****  *****  *****  *****  *****  *****  *****
          |      *****  *****  *****  *****  *****  *****  *****  *****
          |      *****  *****  *****  *****  *****  *****  *****  *****
      20 +       *****  *****  *****  *****  *****  *****  *****  *****
          |      *****  *****  *****  *****  *****  *****  *****  *****
          |      *****  *****  *****  *****  *****  *****  *****  *****
          |      *****  *****  *****  *****  *****  *****  *****  *****
          -------------------------------------------------------------
                  21     23     25     27     29     31     33     35

                              Y MIDPOINT
```

Normal random numbers

It is just as easy to generate numbers with a normal distribution as with a uniform distribution. The random function's name is NORMAL. It produces random numbers from a normal distribution with mean = 0 and standard deviation = 1. To generate numbers, y, from a normal distribution with mean = μ and standard deviation = σ, use the formula

$$y = \mu + \sigma \times x$$

where x is the result from NORMAL. The sample of 40 numbers in Exhibit 11.4 was generated from a normal distribution with mean = 50 and a standard deviation = 10. The program which produced this exhibit was

```
DATA NORMAL;
   DO I = 1 TO 40;
      X = 50 + 10*NORMAL(0);
      OUTPUT;
      END;

PROC CHART DATA=NORMAL;
   VBAR X / MIDPOINTS=20 TO 80 BY 5;
   TITLE 'Sample (n=40) from Normal Distribution';
```

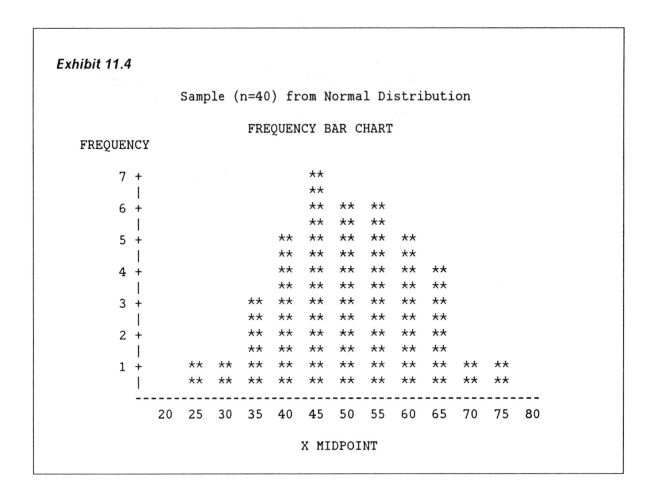

Exhibit 11.4

Sample (n=40) from Normal Distribution

FREQUENCY BAR CHART

GENERATING SAMPLING DISTRIBUTIONS

Imagine now computing the mean of the sample in the preceding section and recording it. Then imagine repeating 500 times this process of random sampling and computing and recording each sample mean. These 500 means themselves form a distribution called the sampling distribution. The result of this process is shown in Exhibit 11.5. At the top of the exhibit are listed the means of the first six samples. In all, 500 such means were computed and then charted, as shown in the lower part of the exhibit. This distribution may be called an empirical sampling distribution since it is based on 500 samples. The theoretical sampling distribution would be based on an infinite number of samples. It can be shown that this theoretical sampling distribution has a normal distribution with mean = 50 and standard deviation $= \dfrac{10}{\sqrt{40}} = 1.58$. You can see from the chart that these values are approximately correct.

Exhibit 11.5

```
            Sampling Distribution: 500 Samples (n=40)

                    SAMPLE       MEAN

                       1       53.6192
                       2       50.3727
                       3       50.9203
                       4       49.3712
                       5       51.4754
                       6       50.9829

                           .  .  .  .  .  .  .

                    FREQUENCY BAR CHART
```

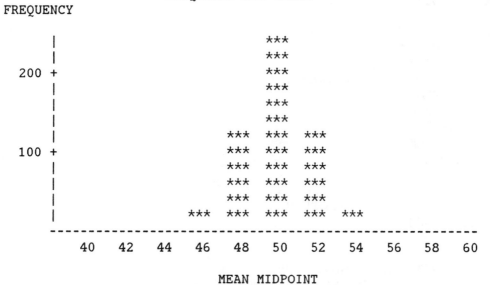

```
FREQUENCY

            |                       ***
            |                       ***
    200  +                          ***
            |                       ***
            |                       ***
            |                       ***
            |             ***   ***   ***
    100  +                ***   ***   ***
            |             ***   ***   ***
            |             ***   ***   ***
            |             ***   ***   ***
            |       ***   ***   ***   ***   ***
            |----------------------------------------------------
           40   42   44   46   48   50   52   54   56   58   60

                        MEAN MIDPOINT
```

Note: The ellipsis points (. . .) denote observations deleted to save space.

A sampling distribution for samples of size 10 will have twice the standard deviation of the previous example. (The standard deviation $= \dfrac{10}{\sqrt{10}} = 3.16$.) See Exhibit 11.6.

Generating a sampling distribution is only slightly more complicated than generating a sample. Two nested DO loops are required. The inner loop generates the sample (as in the previous section) but instead of outputting each random number as it is generated the loop accumulates whatever sum is needed to compute the statistic. When the inner loop is complete, the statistic is computed from the sum and the statistic is output as one observation. The outer loop simply creates more samples. The result is an output data set with one observation for each sample.

For example, here is the program which created the sampling distribution of the mean of samples of size 40 (Exhibit 11.5). There are 500 samples generated and the distribution of the means of these samples is displayed as a frequency distribution.

```
DATA SDIST40;
  N = 40;
  DO SAMPLE = 1 TO 500;
    SUM = 0.0;
    DO I = 1 TO N;
      X = 50 + 10*NORMAL(0);
      SUM = SUM + X;
      END;
    MEAN = SUM / N;
    OUTPUT;
    END;

TITLE 'Sampling Distribution: 500 Samples (n=40)';
PROC PRINT DATA=SDIST40;
  ID SAMPLE;
  VAR MEAN;

PROC CHART DATA=SDIST40;
  VBAR MEAN / MIDPOINTS = 40 TO 60 BY 2;
```

The first statement in the outer loop initializes the sum to zero. Then the sum is accumulated in the inner loop by the statement SUM = SUM + X;. Note that both the initialization and the accumulation are required and cannot be replaced by a sum statement of the form SUM + X;. The latter statement would work only if there were just one sum to be computed. However, there are 500 sums; each of them must be initialized to zero by an explicit assignment statement, SUM =0;.

After the inner loop has concluded, the mean can be computed from the sum by the statement MEAN = SUM / N; and output as an observation. This process is repeated 500 times by the outer loop.

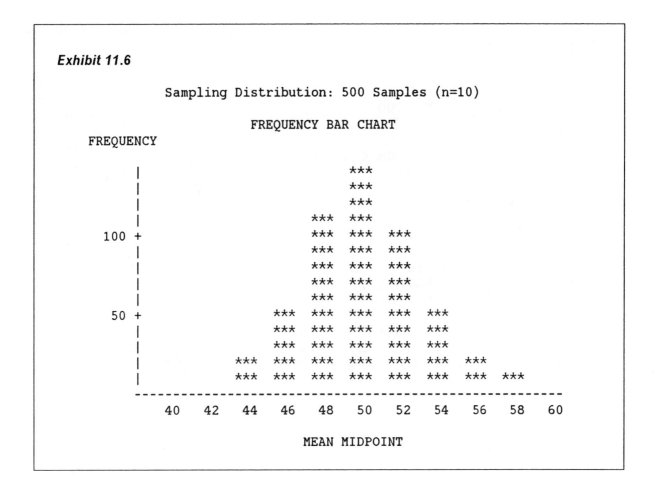

Exhibit 11.6

Sampling Distribution: 500 Samples (n=10)

Essentially the same program (but using N = 10 rather than 40) was used to generate the sampling distribution in Exhibit 11.6:

```
DATA SDIST10;
   N = 10;
   DO SAMPLE = 1 TO 500;
      SUM = 0.0;
      DO I = 1 TO N;
         X = 50 + 10*NORMAL(0);
         SUM = SUM + X;
         END;
      MEAN = SUM / N;
      OUTPUT;
      END;

TITLE 'Sampling Distribution: 500 Samples (n=10)';
PROC CHART DATA=SDIST10;
   VBAR MEAN / MIDPOINTS = 40 TO 60 BY 2;
```

Note that the same midpoints in PROC CHART were used for the two exhibits in order that the two sampling distributions appear on the same scale. In this way the fact that the two distributions have different widths (i.e., different standard deviations) is clearly shown.

Part 3
FORMATTING AND SUBGROUP ANALYSES

Most of the topics and SAS statements introduced in Part 2 have close analogs in conventional programming languages. (Consider, for example, assignment and conditional statements.) The topics in this part are different and give the SAS language a different flavour from other languages. Formats are used in other languages but the concept has been considerably generalized in the SAS language. And the ability to do subgroup analyses with the BY statement is a unique and powerful feature of the SAS language.

Chapter 12

FORMATS

In our discussion of PROC CHART in Chapter 4, we saw that a continuous variable like BIRTHWGT (with many values) must be divided into intervals before creating a chart. In that chapter there were only two ways to do this: either let PROC CHART choose the intervals (usually unsatisfactory) or specify the intervals by midpoints (or number of intervals). Often one wants to do better than this, particularly if the intervals are to have unequal width.

In PROC FREQ (Chapter 5) there is no built-in facility at all for dividing a variable into intervals. The procedure will produce a table with every value of the variable which exists in the data set. For most continuous variables the result is unsatisfactory.

Fortunately, the SAS language provides a general method to divide a variable into intervals. In fact the method, which uses *formats*, is even more general since it allows any set of values of the variable to be combined together to form a group. The method will be illustrated in this chapter by frequency distributions. In later chapters in this part, formats will be used in other contexts as well.

There is a potential source of confusion for readers who are familiar with conventional programming languages such as Fortran, PL/I, Basic, etc. The term "format" is used in these languages to describe how numeric variables are to be printed (e.g., how many decimal places, the use of scientific notation, etc.). The term is also used to describe how character variables are to be printed (e.g., how many leading and trailing blanks). In the SAS language, the term "format" has been generalized greatly.

In the SAS language there are two types of formats: *pre-defined* formats similar to those in other languages and *user-defined* formats which allow a more general grouping. The pre-defined formats, as their name implies, can be used without first defining them; they are supplied with base SAS software. The pre-defined formats are described in the last main section of this chapter. The user-defined formats must first be defined before they are used. Except for the last main section, this chapter concentrates on user-defined formats. Since both types of formats are used in essentially the same way, the description of the use of user-defined formats also applies to the use of pre-defined formats.

There are several potential pitfalls in defining and using formats. The rules described in this chapter are summarized in the SAS Tip.

▶   See SAS Tip 7: *Using formats correctly* (at the end of the chapter).

WHAT IS A FORMAT?

There are two aspects to formats. First, the format has to be defined—this is already done for pre-defined formats but must be done in a PROC FORMAT step for user-defined formats. Second, the format is used—this is done by a FORMAT statement in a PROC step. Suppose, for example, that we have a variable GENDER whose values are 1 (for male) and 2 (for female). When this variable is printed (say by PROC PRINT), the words "Male" and

"Female" are to be printed in place of the original values "1" and "2". Arranging this modification is a two-stage process in the SAS language. In the first stage we have to associate "Male" with "1" and "Female" with "2". This process is called assigning *value labels*. The association is made by a PROC FORMAT step. It is important to note that *no* reference is made to the variable GENDER when this association is made. The PROC FORMAT step simply assigns labels to values and stores this association under a format name specified by the user. The second stage is the PROC PRINT step itself. One of the statements in the PROC PRINT step is a FORMAT statement which states that the variable GENDER is to be printed using the stored format defined in the preceding PROC FORMAT step.

In this example, the two-stage process seems cumbersome. But consider the following extension. Suppose the SAS data set has two other variables GENFR1 and GENFR2, which give the gender (coded 1 and 2) of two friends of the child represented in the observation. We want these variables also to be printed using the value labels "Male" and "Female". The PROC FORMAT step has already defined these value labels so that the format there defined can also be used when GENFR1 and GENFR2 are printed. In summary, the job would consist of a PROC FORMAT step defining one format for printing gender labels and a PROC PRINT step in which a FORMAT statement says that the three variables GENDER, GENFR1, and GENFR2 are to be printed using that format.

Example 1

In its simplest form PROC FORMAT assigns labels to the values of a variable. Here are the PROC steps for the gender example just discussed.

```
PROC FORMAT;
  VALUE GENDFORM
    1 = 'Male'
    2 = 'Female';

PROC PRINT DATA=XXXX;
  VAR NAME GENDER FRIEND1 GENFR1 FRIEND2 GENFR2;
  FORMAT GENDER GENFR1 GENFR2 GENDFORM.;
```

The format is defined by the VALUE statement in the PROC FORMAT step. This statement has been displayed, for clarity, over three lines although it is just one statement (ending in a semi-colon). The first word, following VALUE, is the name of the format (GENDFORM). This is followed by a series of "equations" which state that a value (on the left hand side) is to be given the label (on the right hand side). The format (GENDFORM) is used in the PROC PRINT step. The FORMAT statement lists the three variables and the name of the format used to print their values. Note carefully that *the format name is terminated by a period in the FORMAT statement*. The period (an identifying marker) is needed so that the SAS System knows that GENDFORM is the name of a format and not the name of a variable.[1]

---

[1] In the VALUE statement, an identifying marker is not needed after the format name (and a period must *not* be used) since the SAS System knows that the name after VALUE must be a format name. (The use of a period in formats dates from Fortran in the 1950s.)

Example 2

More commonly, PROC FORMAT assigns labels to intervals of values. In this way values are "grouped", e.g., for forming distributions. The following statements define and then use a format which groups a weight variable into three intervals "Light", "Normal", and "Heavy".

```
PROC FORMAT;
   VALUE WGTFORM LOW-7.5 = 'Light'
                 7.6-9.5 = 'Normal'
                 9.6-HIGH = 'Heavy';

PROC CHART DATA=DEMO;
   VBAR BIRTHWGT / DISCRETE;
   FORMAT BIRTHWGT WGTFORM.;
   TITLE 'Grouping Birth Weight by a Format';
```

The output is shown in Exhibit 12.1. Here the VALUE statement (defining format WGTFORM) gives labels to intervals of values. Note that keywords "LOW" and "HIGH" may be used in these intervals so that the smallest and largest values do not need to be known when a format is defined. The intervals should of course be non-overlapping; they may be specified in any order.

The FORMAT statement in the PROC CHART step associates the format name (WGTFORM) with the variable BIRTHWGT. Note again that the format name is terminated by a period.[2] All values of BIRTHWGT which are less than or equal to 7.5 are grouped in an interval labelled "Light". Similarly the label "Normal" is applied to all values between 7.6 and 9.5 inclusive and the label "Heavy" applies to all values greater than or equal to 9.6.

Note that the DISCRETE option is still required on the VBAR statement even though the variable has been grouped by the FORMAT statement. The reason for this is that the variable remains numeric; PROC CHART carries out its own grouping on numeric variables unless the DISCRETE option is specified. See Chapter 4.

In both these examples we see that the PROC FORMAT step gives a format name to the association of values and labels and that the FORMAT statement associates a format name with one or more variables.

---

[2] It is convenient to use format names including the letters "FORM" or "FMT", but this is not required.

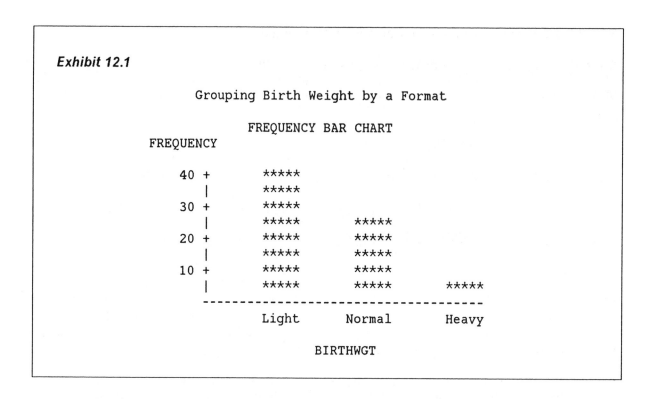

Exhibit 12.1

```
              Grouping Birth Weight by a Format

                        FREQUENCY BAR CHART
          FREQUENCY

             40 +      *****
                |      *****
             30 +      *****
                |      *****         *****
             20 +      *****         *****
                |      *****         *****
             10 +      *****         *****
                |      *****         *****         *****
                ------------------------------------------
                       Light         Normal        Heavy

                             BIRTHWGT
```

PROC FORMAT AND VALUE LABELS

In general a PROC FORMAT step begins with a PROC FORMAT statement and is followed by one or more VALUE statements. Each VALUE statement defines one format. The general form is therefore:

```
PROC FORMAT;
    VALUE formatname range = 'label' range = 'label' . . .;
    VALUE formatname range = 'label' range = 'label' . . .;
    . . .
```

(What we have been calling an interval of values is usually called a "range" in SAS documentation so we use that term here.)

Parts of the VALUE statement

As shown above, each VALUE statement has a name of the format followed by one or more "equations", each of which defines a range of values to have a certain label.

Formatname: *formatname* may be any SAS name, i.e. up to eight characters in length, but *formatname cannot end in a digit.*[3] If the format is for character variables the name must begin with a "$" and can have no more than seven following characters. The *formatname* in a

---

[3] The reason for this restriction relates to features of pre-defined formats. See later in this chapter.

VALUE statement must *not* be terminated with a period.

Range: Ranges may have one of several forms:

Form	*Explanation*
value	A single value
value1–value2	All values in the range from value1 to value2 (inclusive)
value1 < –value2	All values more than value1 and less than or equal to value2
value1– < value2	All values more than or equal to value1 and less than value2
range1, range2	Several ranges (of the above types) may be listed, separated by commas

The values themselves may be any number (or character string for a character format) or may be one of two keywords: LOW or HIGH. LOW and HIGH refer to the smallest and largest possible values, respectively. The keyword OTHER may be used as a range itself to specify any value not included in any other range in the VALUE statement.

Label: A label may be any string of characters (in quotes) up to 40 characters in length. However, some procedures may only use the first 8 or 16 characters.

Examples of VALUE statements

The variable BLOOD in the Statlab data has the following codes:

Code	*Meaning*
1	O, Rh−
2	A, Rh−
3	B, Rh−
4	AB, Rh−
5	O, Rh+
6	A, Rh+
7	B, Rh+
8	AB, Rh+
9	unknown

Exhibit 12.2 shows ways to format the BLOOD variable. The first format (BLVALUE) just assigns value labels to the nine codes. The second (BLLETTER) groups the codes by letter (O, A, B, AB, and unknown). The third (BLRH) groups the codes by Rh factor (RH−, RH+, and unknown).

```
Exhibit 12.2  Formatting BLOOD in Three Ways

PROC FORMAT;
  VALUE BLVALUE
    1 = 'O  RH-'
    2 = 'A  RH-'
    3 = 'B  RH-'
    4 = 'AB RH-'
    5 = 'O  RH+'
    6 = 'A  RH+'
    7 = 'B  RH+'
    8 = 'AB RH+'
    9 = 'Unknown';

  VALUE BLLETTER
    1,5 = 'O'
    2,6 = 'A'
    3,7 = 'B'
    4,8 = 'AB'
    9 = 'Unknown';

  VALUE BLRH
    1-4 = 'RH-'
    5-8 = 'RH+'
    9 = 'Unknown';
```

THE FORMAT STATEMENT

The FORMAT statement has the form:

  FORMAT *variables formatname* . . .;

In this statement, one or more variable names are followed by a format name. The values of each of these variables are to be grouped by the format. Several sets of "*variables formatname*" may follow one another on one FORMAT statement (or several FORMAT statements may be used). The *formatname* in a FORMAT statement *must* include a period.

Here we show some examples of PROC steps with FORMAT statements. (The FORMAT statement can also be used in a DATA step—see Chapter 16.)

Example 1

Exhibit 12.3 shows the variable BLOOD formatted by BLVALUE. The PROC step for this exhibit is:

```
PROC PRINT DATA=DEMO;
  VAR FAMILY BLOOD;
  FORMAT BLOOD BLVALUE.;
  TITLE 'Formatting of BLOOD by BLVALUE';
```

Exhibit 12.3

Formatting of BLOOD by BLVALUE

OBS	FAMILY	BLOOD	
1	11-21	B	RH+
2	11-51	O	RH+
3	12-21	O	RH+
4	12-51	O	RH-
5	13-21	B	RH+
6	13-51	A	RH+
7	14-21	O	RH+
8	14-51	A	RH+
9	15-21	A	RH+

. . . .

Note: The ellipsis points (. . .) denote observations deleted to save space.

Example 2

Exhibit 12.4 shows the variable BLOOD formatted by BLLETTER. The PROC step for this exhibit is:

```
PROC PRINT DATA=DEMO;
   VAR FAMILY BLOOD;
   FORMAT BLOOD BLLETTER.;
   TITLE 'Formatting of BLOOD by BLLETTER';
```

Exhibit 12.4

```
                Formatting of BLOOD by BLLETTER

            OBS      FAMILY      BLOOD

             1       11-21         B
             2       11-51         O
             3       12-21         O
             4       12-51         O
             5       13-21         B
             6       13-51         A
             7       14-21         O
             8       14-51         A
             9       15-21         A
                     . . . . . . .
```

Note: The ellipsis points (. . .) denote observations deleted to save space.

Example 3

Exhibit 12.5 shows the variable BLOOD formatted by BLRH. The PROC step for this exhibit is:

```
PROC PRINT DATA=DEMO;
   VAR FAMILY BLOOD;
   FORMAT BLOOD BLRH.;
   TITLE 'Formatting of BLOOD by BLRH';
```

```
Exhibit 12.5

                  Formatting of BLOOD by BLRH

            OBS      FAMILY       BLOOD

             1       11-21        RH+
             2       11-51        RH+
             3       12-21        RH+
             4       12-51        RH-
             5       13-21        RH+
             6       13-51        RH+
             7       14-21        RH+
             8       14-51        RH+
             9       15-21        RH+

                      . . . . . . .
```

Note: The ellipsis points (. . .) denote observations deleted to save space.

Example 4

Exhibit 12.6 shows the output from PROC CHART when BLOOD is formatted by BLVALUE. The PROC step for this exhibit is:

```
PROC CHART DATA=DEMO;
   VBAR BLOOD / DISCRETE;
   FORMAT BLOOD BLVALUE.;
   TITLE 'PROC CHART with a Format';
```

Just as in Exhibit 12.1, the DISCRETE option is needed since the variable, although formatted, remains numeric.

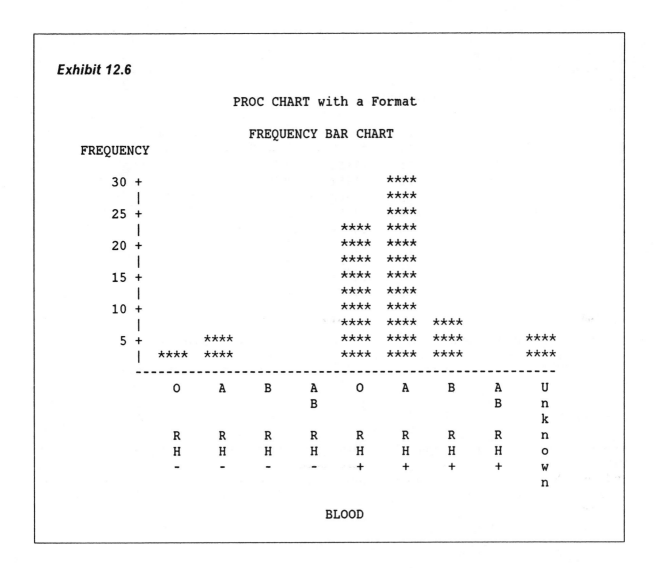

Exhibit 12.6

```
                     PROC CHART with a Format

                     FREQUENCY BAR CHART

FREQUENCY


   30 +                                    ****
      |                                    ****
   25 +                                    ****
      |                             ****   ****
   20 +                             ****   ****
      |                             ****   ****
   15 +                             ****   ****
      |                             ****   ****
   10 +                             ****   ****
      |                             ****   ****   ****
    5 +           ****              ****   ****   ****            ****
      |    ****   ****              ****   ****   ****            ****
      -------------------------------------------------------------------
            O      A      B      A      O      A      B      A      U
                                 B                           B      n
                                                                    k
            R      R      R      R      R      R      R      R      n
            H      H      H      H      H      H      H      H      o
            -      -      -      -      +      +      +      +      w
                                                                    n

                                 BLOOD
```

Example 5

Exhibit 12.7 shows the output from PROC FREQ when BLOOD is formatted by BLLETTER. The PROC step for this exhibit is:

```
PROC FREQ DATA=DEMO;
   TABLES BLOOD;
   FORMAT BLOOD BLLETTER.;
   TITLE 'PROC FREQ with a Format';
```

```
Exhibit 12.7

                    PROC FREQ with a Format

                                        CUMULATIVE    CUMULATIVE
        BLOOD    FREQUENCY    PERCENT    FREQUENCY     PERCENT
        -----------------------------------------------------------
        O             24       33.3          24         33.3
        A             33       45.8          57         79.2
        B              8       11.1          65         90.3
        AB             2        2.8          67         93.1
        Unknown        5        6.9          72        100.0
```

FORMATS FOR CHARACTER VARIABLES

As previously noted, there are just two changes needed when a character variable is formatted:

• The *formatname* must begin with a "$" and have no more than seven following characters, and

• The values in the VALUE statement must be enclosed in quotes.

Suppose an external file has a variable SEX coded as a character variable with values "M" and "F". Suppose that it is desired to print the values by the labels "Male" and "Female". Here is a short SAS program which reads NAME (also character) and SEX and prints the data set:

```
DATA TOYFMT;
  INPUT NAME $ SEX $;
  LINES;
  Robert      M
  Joan        F
  Anne        F
;

PROC FORMAT;
  VALUE $SEXFMT
    'M' = 'Male'
    'F' = 'Female';

PROC PRINT DATA=TOYFMT;
  FORMAT SEX $SEXFMT.;
  TITLE 'Output from a Format for a Character Variable';
```

The output is shown in Exhibit 12.8.

Exhibit 12.8

Output from a Format for a Character Variable

```
OBS      NAME      SEX

 1       Robert    Male
 2       Joan      Female
 3       Anne      Female
```

Note that the format name "$SEXFMT" begins with a "$" and that the values, "M" and "F", are in quotes in the VALUE statement. Finally note that if the variable SEX had been coded "1" and "2" instead of "M" and "F" and *if the variable had still been considered as a character variable* (as it might reasonably be considered to be since the values are just codes, not numbers on which calculations can be done), then the values in the value statement would still have to be in quotes:

```
PROC FORMAT;
   VALUE $SEXFMT
      '1' = 'Male'
      '2' = 'Female';
```

See SAS Tip 3: *Deciding whether a variable is numeric or character* in Chapter 2.

PRE-DEFINED FORMATS

There are several dozen pre-defined formats available in base SAS software. Their principal use is for printing numbers with a specified number of decimal places and with a specified (or maximum) field width. However, as we noted at the beginning of the chapter, a format in SAS language is a grouping of values of a variable as well as simply providing a transformation between the internal representation of a value (as stored in a data set) and its external representation (as printed). These various aspects of formats will be illustrated in this section for the pre-defined formats.

We describe here five numeric formats and one character format. Each format specifies a field width "w" and three of them specify the number of places of decimals "d". The numeric formats are:

w.d   Standard numeric format

BESTw.   Best format (the SAS System chooses the best form for the number)

COMMAw.d   Comma format (commas separate every three digits; *d* may only be 0 or 2)

DOLLARw.d   Dollar format (same as comma format with "$" preceding value)

Ew.   Scientific format (number times 10 to a power)

The character format is:

$w.   Standard character format

Here is a short program to illustrate the formats:

```
DATA SHOWFMT;
  A = 87654.321;
  B = A; C = A; D = A; E = A; F = A; G = A; H = A;
  I = 'SAS Formats';

PROC PRINT DATA=SHOWFMT;
  TITLE 'Examples of Pre-defined Formats';
  VAR A B C D E F G H I;
  FORMAT A 12.2
         B 7.2
         C BEST7.
         D 4.2
         E COMMA12.2
         F DOLLAR12.
         G DOLLAR.
         H E12.
         I $5.;
```

Exhibit 12.9 shows the output.

Exhibit 12.9

```
              Examples of Pre-defined Formats

   OBS        A          B          C          D          E

    1     87654.32    87654.3    87654.3      88E3    87,654.32

   OBS        F          G          H          I

    1     $87,654     87654    8.76543E+04    SAS F
```

Before explaining why each value printed as it did in the exhibit, we state the general rules for pre-defined formats.

Field width

- If the field width *w* is specified in the format, the field in which the value prints is at most *w* columns wide. If the value needs only a smaller field, the leading blanks are trimmed. This allows PROC PRINT, for example, to print values in minimum space.

- If the field width *w* is not specified, a default value is used: 12 for the BEST. and E. formats, 6 for COMMA. and DOLLAR., and the length of the variable for $.. Note that the *w* may not be omitted from the w.d format.

- If the numeric value cannot fit in the field width specified or assumed by default, the BEST. format is used (with the same field width). If the BEST. format can't print the number without misrepresentation, asterisks are printed instead.

- The maximum value of *w* is 32 for the numeric formats and 200 for the character formats. The minimum value is 1 for w.d, BEST., and $.; 2 for COMMA. and DOLLAR.; 7 for E..

- Numeric values are always right-justified in the field; character values are always left-justified in the field.

- The field width *w* plays a somewhat different role in the E.w format. If the width is great enough, positive numbers are printed in the form 8.353E+04 and negative numbers in the form −8.353E+04. (Of course the power of 10 may be negative in either case.) In fact, the number of decimal places printed depends on *w*: negative numbers are printed to fill *w* columns and positive numbers are printed to fill *w* − 1 columns (leaving a blank where the negative sign would go). For example, if the number is −83530, it will print as −8.353E+04 in format E10., and will print as −8.3530000E+04 in format E14.. If the width is not great enough, the decimals or the "+0" in the exponent are omitted in order to represent the number in the specified field width. Of course, a negative sign of the number or a negative exponent is never omitted.

Number of decimals

- The number of decimals *d* is used only with the w.d, COMMA., and DOLLAR. formats. If specified for w.d, the value of *d* must be less than *w*. For COMMA. and DOLLAR., the value of *d* must be either 0 or 2.

- If *d* is omitted, zero is assumed: no decimals are printed nor is the decimal point printed.

No format

- If no format is specified, the BEST. format is used for numeric variables (with field width 12) and the $. format is used for character variables (with field width equal to the length of the variable).

Explanation of exhibit

We now return to Exhibit 12.9 and explain the output for each variable.

- Variable A in format 12.2 is printed as expected with two places of decimals.
- Variable B in format 7.2 is printed with only one decimal place since there is not enough room in a field width of seven for two decimal places. The SAS System has changed the format to BEST. and has done the best it could in seven columns.
- Variable C in format BEST7. gives the same result as format 7.2.
- Variable D in format 4.2 shows what BEST. (to which the format has been changed) does in a very small field width—the SAS System uses scientific notation, representing the number as 88×10^3, the best it can do in four columns.
- Variable E in format COMMA12.2 is printed with commas to mark the thousands.
- Variable F in format DOLLAR12. is similar except that a dollar sign is used and, in this case, no decimals are printed.
- Variable G in format DOLLAR. is printed in a default width of six which doesn't leave room for either the dollar sign or the comma.
- Variable H in format E12. is printed in scientific notation—the number is represented as 8.76543×10^4. Note that this positive number is printed in 11 columns (leaving a blank where the minus sign would go); the number of significant digits is determined by this width.
- Variable I in format $5. is printed with only the first five characters of its value since the field width was specified as five.

Formats in PROC steps

We have just shown how pre-defined formats can be used in PROC PRINT. In the earlier sections of this chapter, several examples were given of user-defined formats not only in PROC PRINT but also in PROCs CHART and FREQ. Pre-defined formats are only rarely used in such PROC steps. We give an example of such use to emphasize a theme of this chapter that formats, including the pre-defined ones, just divide the values of a variable into groups.

The following program provides a frequency table of the Statlab birth weights, to the nearest pound. Without the format (which specifies zero places of decimals) the output from PROC FREQ would have a separate line for each decimal value (7.1, 7.2, etc.).

```
PROC FREQ DATA=DEMO;
   TABLES BIRTHWGT;
   FORMAT BIRTHWGT 8.;
   TITLE 'Table of Birth Weights, to the Nearest Pound';
```

The output is shown in Exhibit 12.10.

Exhibit 12.10

Table of Birth Weights, to the Nearest Pound

BIRTHWGT	FREQUENCY	PERCENT	CUMULATIVE FREQUENCY	CUMULATIVE PERCENT
5	2	2.8	2	2.8
6	10	13.9	12	16.7
7	25	34.7	37	51.4
8	18	25.0	55	76.4
9	10	13.9	65	90.3
10	7	9.7	72	100.0

Formats in PUT statements

Formats may be used directly in PUT statements. Recall from Chapter 10 that in *list style* the value is written in the columns following the current line pointer and one blank column is left after the value. In *column style*, the actual columns in which the value is to be written are specified. Finally, in *named output*, the written value is preceded by the variable name and an equals sign.

Formatted style, described here, allows the programmer to specify yet more precisely how the value is to be written. The variable name on the PUT statement is followed by the format (either pre-defined or user-defined) to be used. There is one difference in the interpretation of pre-defined formats in PUT statements from the rules previously described: the specified field width is honoured when the value is written. Blank columns are inserted to fill out the field but no extra blanks are inserted between fields unless specified by the programmer. Of course, as previously noted, when the Ew. format is used, the number is printed in the full field width anyway.

Named output may be combined with formatted style by following the variable name by an equals sign and then the format. When named output is used, leading blanks are trimmed just as they are when formats are used in procedures. Hence there are only two situations where the full width specified in the format is used: in the Ew. format and in formatted style (without named output).

We illustrate formatted style by the following variation of Exhibit 12.9:

```
DATA SHOWFMT;
  A = 87654.321;
  B = A; C = A; D = A; E = A; F = A; G = A; H = A;
  I = 'SAS Formats';
  FILE PRINT;
  TITLE 'Examples of Formatted Style in a PUT Statement';
  PUT;
  PUT A 12.2      @20
      B 7.2       @40
      C BEST7.    //
      D 4.2
      E COMMA12.2
      F DOLLAR12.
      G DOLLAR.   //
      H= E12.
      I= $5.;
```

Here all variables are written in formatted style. In addition, named output is used for the last two variables. Only pre-defined formats are illustrated, but user-defined formats may also be used in PUT statements. The output is shown in Exhibit 12.11.

Exhibit 12.11

```
        Examples of Formatted Style in a PUT Statement

      87654.32        87654.3              87654.3

88E3    87,654.32      $87,654 87654

H=8.76543E+04 I=SAS F
```

Explanation of exhibit

- Variable A in format 12.2 prints in a field of width 12.
- Variable B's field starts in column 20; the value fills the field of width 7, leaving only space for one decimal even though the format is 7.2.
- Variable C's field starts in column 40. The result is the same as for B.
- Variables D, E, F, and G print in their respective fields. The characters printed are exactly the same as in Exhibit 12.9.
- Variables H and I illustrate named output. Note that variable H prints in a field of 11 columns even though the specified field width is 12—the leading blank has been trimmed.

SAS Tip 7 Using Formats Correctly

For reference, we repeat some of the rules which have been stated in this chapter. In the author's experience, many errors and difficulties can be traced to problems with formats. The reasons for the rules, in the context of the overall design of the SAS System, are summarized here as well.

When is the period used in the formatname?

The *formatname* appears in a VALUE statement (when a format is defined) and in FORMAT and PUT statements (when a format is used). A period must *not* be used in a VALUE statement. A period *must* be used in FORMAT and PUT statements. The distinction can be explained as follows. In the VALUE statement, the word following "VALUE" must be a *formatname* and hence does not need a period to be identified. However, in the FORMAT and PUT statements, if the *formatname* did not have a period, it could be confused with a variable name. Note that both user-defined and pre-defined formats can be used in FORMAT and PUT statements; the pre-defined formats all have periods anyway (w.d, Ew., DOLLARw.d, etc.), sometimes not even at the end of the format.

What names can be used for user-defined formatnames?

A user-defined *formatname* must be a SAS name (Chapter 3), but certain SAS names are not allowed. Recall that a SAS name may be a single word of from 1 to 8 characters, the first of which must be a letter (A to Z) or an underscore (_). The characters after the first may be letters, digits (0 to 9), or underscores. The restrictions on *formatnames* defined in a VALUE statement are:

1. The *formatname* cannot end in a digit. (Only pre-defined *formatnames* can end in a digit.)

2. *Formatnames* for character variables must have "$" as their first character and can have no more than seven following characters. (The "$" is used by the SAS System to distinguish character from numeric formats.)

What should I watch out for in writing VALUE statements?

1. As stated above, the *formatname* must not have a period.

2. The *formatname* must begin with a "$" if a character format is being defined.

3. Only one semi-colon is used for each VALUE statement; do not use a semi-colon between the successive *range* = '*label*' parts; place a semi-colon at the end of the VALUE statement.

4. The *label* is always quoted. (The *label* is the transformed value and is always considered to be a character string.)

5. The *range* is not quoted if a numeric format is being defined, but is quoted if a character format is being defined. (The *range* is one or more values before transformation; hence the values must be represented in their original form, either numeric or character.)

Chapter 13

SORTING

In order to use the general method available in the SAS System for analyses by subgroup, the SAS data set must be sorted. In this chapter we explain what sorting is and describe the statements needed to sort a data set. The following chapter illustrates various analyses using this general method.

PROC SORT

Sorting is similar to the process in which words are arranged in alphabetical order in a dictionary or in a telephone book. Letters, and therefore words, have a standard ascending order. Similarly numbers may be arranged or sorted in ascending order (from smallest to largest). Alternatively, sorting may be done in reverse or descending order: z comes before y comes before x, . . . or, with numbers, the numbers are arranged from largest to smallest.

Consider first what it means for the Statlab data to be sorted by SEX. This variable is actually numeric: 1 is the code for males and 2 is the code for females. When the data are sorted by SEX, all observations with code 1 appear first, followed by all observations with code 2. The sorted data set is shown in Exhibit 13.1. Even though the formatted values are printed, it is the unformatted (original) values which are actually sorted. Hence males (code 1) appear before females (code 2). Another variable in the data set, MOTHEDUC, is also shown. Note that this variable is not sorted.

It is important to realize that although the data set is sorted on one variable, it is the observations (and not just the values of that variable) that are re-ordered. The first observation in Exhibit 13.1 might have been, say, the 45th observation in the original data set. The first observation in the new data set still corresponds to a single family; all variables have the same values as the variables had for the 45th observation in the original data set.

A data set may be sorted by more than one variable. Suppose we want a listing of the Statlab data in which the observations are sorted by MOTHEDUC but, in addition, within each educational subgroup the observations are sorted by SEX (of child). Such a sort is shown in Exhibit 13.2. In addition we have sorted SEX in "descending" order, that is code 2 (females) before code 1 (males). In effect, values of MOTHEDUC form the major category and values of SEX form the minor category (within the major category).

Statements for PROC SORT

Arranging a sort in the SAS language is easy. The statements are:

> PROC SORT DATA = *SASdataset* [OUT = *SASdataset*];
>   BY *variables*;

As usual, the input data set is specified by the DATA = option. The OUT = option is used to specify the output (sorted) data set. In all the examples in this chapter and the next, the

---

Exhibit 13.1

```
                    Sort by Sex of Child

            OBS     FAMILY        SEX       MOTHEDUC

             1      41-21        Male       Grade 8-12
             2      41-51        Male       Grade 8-12
             3      42-21        Male       HS Grad.
             4      42-51        Male       HS Grad.
             5      43-21        Male       Some Coll.
                        .  .  .  .  .  .
            32      64-51        Male       HS Grad.
            33      65-21        Male       Grade 8-12
            34      65-51        Male       Coll. Grad.
            35      66-21        Male       HS Grad.
            36      66-51        Male       HS Grad.
            37      11-21        Female     HS Grad.
            38      11-51        Female     HS Grad.
            39      12-21        Female     Some Coll.
            40      12-51        Female     HS Grad.
            41      13-21        Female     HS Grad.
                        .  .  .  .  .  .
            68      34-51        Female     HS Grad.
            69      35-21        Female     Some Coll.
            70      35-51        Female     <Grade 8
            71      36-21        Female     Grade 8-12
            72      36-51        Female     Some Coll.
```

Note: The ellipsis points (. . .) denote observations deleted to save space.

---

output data set is specified. However, sometimes it is convenient not to specify it, in which case the input data set is overwritten with the sorted data set.[1]

One or more variables may be specified on the BY statement. If more than one is specified, the values of the first variable form the major grouping of the data set. Within each value of the first variable the data set is sorted by values of the second variable. And so on for third and further variables on the BY statement.

---

[1] You can't omit the OUT= option if the input data set is a permanent data set which can't be overwritten. In that event you will get an error message and the PROC SORT will fail.

Exhibit 13.2

Sort by Mother's Education and by Sex of Child
(Females before Males)

OBS	FAMILY	SEX	MOTHEDUC
1	35-51	Female	<Grade 8
2	62-51	Male	<Grade 8
3	13-51	Female	Grade 8-12
4	21-21	Female	Grade 8-12
5	32-21	Female	Grade 8-12
6	36-21	Female	Grade 8-12
7	41-21	Male	Grade 8-12
8	41-51	Male	Grade 8-12
9	46-21	Male	Grade 8-12
10	51-21	Male	Grade 8-12
11	53-21	Male	Grade 8-12
12	61-21	Male	Grade 8-12
13	65-21	Male	Grade 8-12
	. . . .		
58	14-21	Female	Coll. Grad.
59	21-51	Female	Coll. Grad.
60	22-51	Female	Coll. Grad.
61	25-21	Female	Coll. Grad.
62	25-51	Female	Coll. Grad.
63	26-51	Female	Coll. Grad.
64	31-21	Female	Coll. Grad.
65	33-21	Female	Coll. Grad.
66	33-51	Female	Coll. Grad.
67	52-21	Male	Coll. Grad.
68	56-51	Male	Coll. Grad.
69	63-21	Male	Coll. Grad.
70	63-51	Male	Coll. Grad.
71	64-21	Male	Coll. Grad.
72	65-51	Male	Coll. Grad.

Note: The ellipsis points (. . .) denote observations deleted to save space.

Exhibit 13.1 was produced by the following PROC steps:

```
PROC SORT DATA=DEMO OUT=SORT1;
  BY SEX;

PROC FORMAT;
  VALUE SEXFORM
    1 = 'Male'
    2 = 'Female'
    ;
  VALUE MEDFORM
    0 = '<Grade 8'
    1 = 'Grade 8-12'
    2 = 'HS Grad.'
    3 = 'Some Coll.'
    4 = 'Coll. Grad.'
    ;

PROC PRINT DATA=SORT1;
  VAR FAMILY SEX MOTHEDUC;
  FORMAT SEX SEXFORM. MOTHEDUC MEDFORM.;
  TITLE 'Sort by Sex of Child';
```

Here just one variable is sorted.

Sorting in descending order

Any variable on the BY statement may be preceded by "DESCENDING" to make the sort in descending order of that variable. Hence a more complete form of the BY statement is:

BY [DESCENDING] *variable* . . .;

where ". . ." indicates that the pair "[DESCENDING] *variable*" may be repeated.

Exhibit 13.2 illustrated such a sort; it was produced by the following PROC steps:

```
PROC SORT DATA=DEMO OUT=SORT2;
  BY MOTHEDUC DESCENDING SEX;

PROC PRINT DATA=SORT2;
  VAR FAMILY SEX MOTHEDUC;
  FORMAT SEX SEXFORM. MOTHEDUC MEDFORM.;
  TITLE "Sort by Mother's Education and by Sex of Child";
  TITLE2 '(Females before Males)';
```

Here the sort is by two variables MOTHEDUC and SEX. MOTHEDUC is the major category and SEX is the minor category. Two variations have been made from the previous exhibit: first, SEX is sorted in descending order, and, second, the variables have been specified in the opposite order (SEX and MOTHEDUC) on the VAR statement in PROC PRINT. The VAR statement does not affect the sorting (which has been completed before the PROC PRINT step begins). The VAR statement only affects the order of the columns on the printed page.

Chapter 14

ANALYSIS BY SUBGROUPS

There are three main reasons for sorting a data set. You may simply want to produce a printed list in sorted order (as in the exhibits of the previous chapter). Certain "data set operations" such as merging and updating data sets, not discussed in this book, require sorted data sets. Finally, a very common use of a sorted data set in the SAS System is to carry out an analysis by subgroups. In this use, the fact that the data set is sorted in alphabetic or numeric order is not the essential property of the sort. The essential property is that the data set is divided into subsets (or subgroups), each of which has the same value of the BY variable.[1] These subsets are called *BY groups*. If the sort has been done with two (or more) BY variables then all observations in a BY group have the same values of all the BY variables.

USING THE BY STATEMENT IN PROC STEPS

Once a data set has been divided into BY groups it can be analyzed by subgroups by simply adding a BY statement to the PROC step for that procedure. The BY statement has the same form as it has with PROC SORT:

> BY [DESCENDING] *variable . . .;*

We now show some examples of subgroup analyses with PROCs CHART, MEANS, and UNIVARIATE.

Tables and charts of frequencies

Exhibit 14.1 was produced by the following statements:

```
PROC SORT DATA=DEMO OUT=SORTSEX;
  BY SEX;

PROC CHART DATA=SORTSEX;
  VBAR BIRTHWGT / DISCRETE;
  TITLE 'Two Frequency Graphs';
  BY SEX;
  FORMAT SEX SEXFORM. BIRTHWGT WGTFORM.;
```

---

[1] In fact, it is possible to analyze an *unsorted* data set by subgroups provided that all observations with a common value of a variable (or common values of several variables) appear consecutively in the data set. In this case the data set is not sorted in alphabetic or numeric order but yet can be analyzed by subgroups. See the *SAS User's Guide* for details.

The result is essentially the same as if the data set had been split in two (one data set for males and one for females) and the two data sets analyzed separately. But the method of BY-group analysis is a very convenient way to carry out such analyses.[2]

Note that in this analysis there are two PROC steps (in addition to the PROC FORMAT step which creates the formats): the PROC SORT step sorts the data set into BY groups and the PROC CHART step uses the sorted data set. It is important to observe that a BY statement must be included with *each* of the two steps. If the BY statement were omitted in the PROC CHART step a single chart would be produced for the whole data set.

Exhibit 14.2 was produced by the following statements:

```
PROC FREQ DATA=SORTSEX;
  TABLES BIRTHWGT;
  FORMAT SEX SEXFORM. BIRTHWGT WGTFORM.;
  TITLE 'Two Tables of One-way Frequencies';
  BY SEX;
```

(The sorted data set and the formats from the preceding program were used here.) The TABLES, FORMAT, TITLE, and BY statements following the PROC FREQ statement may appear in any order. In general, the statements following any PROC statement may appear in any order.

In this example there is a way to get a better tabular representation; furthermore sorting is not required. This is the two-way frequency table shown in Exhibit 14.3, which was produced by these statements:

```
PROC FREQ DATA=DEMO;
  TABLES SEX*BIRTHWGT;
  FORMAT SEX SEXFORM. BIRTHWGT WGTFORM.;
  TITLE 'Two-way Frequency Table';
```

There is often more than one way to carry out essentially the same analysis. Compare Exhibits 14.2 and 14.3. The subgroup frequencies are produced by either analysis. However, producing the two-way analysis directly in Exhibit 14.3 is easier to specify (since the PROC SORT step is not needed), is more efficient (since a sort of a large data set requires significant computer resources), and produces a more comprehensive analysis (note the marginal totals).[3]

---

[2] Formats for Exhibits 14.1, 14.2, and 14.3:

```
PROC FORMAT;
  VALUE SEXFORM
    1 = 'Male'
    2 = 'Female'
    ;
  VALUE WGTFORM
    4.5<-6.0 = '4.5<-6'
    6.0<-7.5 = '6<-7.5'
    7.5<-9.0 = '7.5<-9'
    9.0<-10.5 = '9<-10.5'
    ;
```

[3] An additional point: further statistical analysis can be carried out on a two-way table which cannot be done on

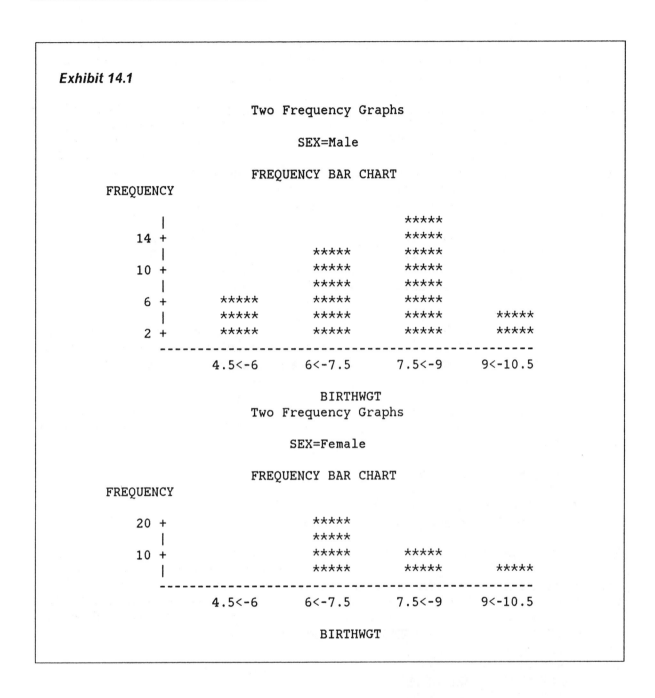

Exhibit 14.1

```
                        Two Frequency Graphs

                             SEX=Male

                       FREQUENCY BAR CHART

    FREQUENCY

            |                                     *****
         14 +                                     *****
            |                         *****        *****
         10 +                         *****        *****
            |                         *****        *****
          6 +           *****         *****        *****
            |           *****         *****        *****        *****
          2 +           *****         *****        *****        *****
            -----------------------------------------------------------
                      4.5<-6        6<-7.5       7.5<-9       9<-10.5

                             BIRTHWGT
                        Two Frequency Graphs

                             SEX=Female

                       FREQUENCY BAR CHART

    FREQUENCY

         20 +                         *****
            |                         *****
         10 +                         *****        *****
            |                         *****        *****        *****
            -----------------------------------------------------------
                      4.5<-6        6<-7.5       7.5<-9       9<-10.5

                             BIRTHWGT
```

Of course, a subgroup analysis using BY groups is often the only way such an analysis can be performed. PROCs CHART and FREQ have built-in features for subgroup analysis, but most other PROCs do not have such features. Subgroup analyses can still be carried out by sorting the data set and using the BY statement in the PROC. This flexibility is an outstanding feature of the SAS language. (See last example in this chapter, using PROC UNIVARIATE.)

---

two separate one-way tables.

Exhibit 14.2

                              Two Tables of One-way Frequencies

                                          SEX=Male

                                                      CUMULATIVE   CUMULATIVE
             BIRTHWGT   FREQUENCY   PERCENT   FREQUENCY   PERCENT

             4.5<-6   5   13.9   5   13.9
             6<-7.5   12   33.3   17   47.2
             7.5<-9   15   41.7   32   88.9
             9<-10.5   4   11.1   36   100.0
                              Two Tables of One-way Frequencies

                                         SEX=Female

                                                      CUMULATIVE   CUMULATIVE
             BIRTHWGT   FREQUENCY   PERCENT   FREQUENCY   PERCENT

             4.5<-6   1   2.8   1   2.8
             6<-7.5   22   61.1   23   63.9
             7.5<-9   8   22.2   31   86.1
             9<-10.5   5   13.9   36   100.0

Tables and charts of means

Exhibit 14.4 was produced by the following statements:

```
PROC SORT DATA=DEMO OUT=SORTEDUC;
  BY MOTHEDUC;

PROC MEANS DATA=SORTEDUC MAXDEC=2 N MEAN;
  VAR BIRTHWGT;
  BY MOTHEDUC;
  FORMAT MOTHEDUC MEDFORM.;
  TITLE 'Table of Means';
```

Exhibit 14.3

```
                    Two-way Frequency Table

                 TABLE OF SEX BY BIRTHWGT

   SEX        BIRTHWGT

   FREQUENCY|
    PERCENT |
    ROW PCT |
    COL PCT |4.5<-6  |6<-7.5  |7.5<-9  |9<-10.5 |   TOTAL
   ---------+--------+--------+--------+--------+
   Male     |      5 |     12 |     15 |      4 |     36
            |   6.94 |  16.67 |  20.83 |   5.56 |  50.00
            |  13.89 |  33.33 |  41.67 |  11.11 |
            |  83.33 |  35.29 |  65.22 |  44.44 |
   ---------+--------+--------+--------+--------+
   Female   |      1 |     22 |      8 |      5 |     36
            |   1.39 |  30.56 |  11.11 |   6.94 |  50.00
            |   2.78 |  61.11 |  22.22 |  13.89 |
            |  16.67 |  64.71 |  34.78 |  55.56 |
   ---------+--------+--------+--------+--------+
   TOTAL           6       34       23        9        72
                8.33    47.22    31.94    12.50   100.00
```

Exhibit 14.4

```
                              Table of Means

                   VARIABLE              N            MEAN

                   -------- MOTHEDUC=<Grade 8 --------

                   BIRTHWGT              2             5.75

                   ------- MOTHEDUC=Grade 8-12 -------

                   BIRTHWGT             11             6.95

                   -------- MOTHEDUC=HS Grad. --------

                   BIRTHWGT             26             7.93

                   ------- MOTHEDUC=Some Coll. -------

                   BIRTHWGT             18             7.73

                   ------ MOTHEDUC=Coll. Grad. -------

                   BIRTHWGT             15             7.34
```

In this case too we can get the same results in another way. Exhibit 14.5 displays the same means as shown in Exhibit 14.4 but the former does not require a sort whereas the latter does.[4] Exhibit 14.5 was produced by these statements:

```
PROC CHART DATA=DEMO;
   VBAR MOTHEDUC / DISCRETE SUMVAR=BIRTHWGT TYPE=MEAN;
   FORMAT MOTHEDUC MEDFORM.;
   TITLE 'Graph of Means';
```

---

[4] Format for Exhibits 14.4 and 14.5:

```
PROC FORMAT;
   VALUE MEDFORM
      0 = '<Grade 8'
      1 = 'Grade 8-12'
      2 = 'HS Grad.'
      3 = 'Some Coll.'
      4 = 'Coll. Grad.'
      ;
```

```
Exhibit 14.5

                            Graph of Means

                          BAR CHART OF MEANS
     BIRTHWGT MEAN

     8 +                                *****
       |                                *****       *****       *****
       |                    *****       *****       *****       *****
       |                    *****       *****       *****       *****
     6 +                    *****       *****       *****       *****
       |        *****       *****       *****       *****       *****
       |        *****       *****       *****       *****       *****
       |        *****       *****       *****       *****       *****
     4 +        *****       *****       *****       *****       *****
       |        *****       *****       *****       *****       *****
       |        *****       *****       *****       *****       *****
       |        *****       *****       *****       *****       *****
     2 +        *****       *****       *****       *****       *****
       |        *****       *****       *****       *****       *****
       |        *****       *****       *****       *****       *****
       |        *****       *****       *****       *****       *****
       |
       -------------------------------------------------------------------
             <Grade 8   Grade 8-12    HS Grad.   Some Coll. Coll. Grad.

                               MOTHEDUC
```

Example of PROC UNIVARIATE

Exhibit 14.6 shows an analysis of the PEABODY variable separately for males and females. This analysis by PROC UNIVARIATE was produced by the following statements:

```
PROC UNIVARIATE DATA=SORTSEX;
   VAR PEABODY;
   BY SEX;
   FORMAT SEX SEXFORM.;
   TITLE 'Analysis of PEABODY by SEX';
```

(The format was defined in a preceding footnote.)

Exhibit 14.6

```
                 Analysis of PEABODY by SEX

                         SEX=Male

                        UNIVARIATE

  VARIABLE=PEABODY


                         MOMENTS

       N                 36  SUM WGTS            36
       MEAN        77.5556  SUM               2792
       STD DEV     8.56386  VARIANCE       73.3397
       SKEWNESS  -.00107513  KURTOSIS     -0.306593
             .   .   .   .   .   .   .

                        SEX=Female

                        UNIVARIATE

  VARIABLE=PEABODY


                         MOMENTS

       N                 36  SUM WGTS            36
       MEAN          77.5  SUM               2790
       STD DEV     8.03386  VARIANCE       64.5429
       SKEWNESS   0.0768368  KURTOSIS     -0.112711
             .   .   .   .   .   .   .
```

Note: The ellipsis points (. . .) denote observations deleted to save space.

Chapter 15

CUSTOMIZED REPORTS

The PRINT procedure is a very useful, flexible program, but in some cases it cannot create the printed report you want. Consider the task of calculating the mean birth length and mean birth weight separately for children of each sex. You could of course get the means from PROC MEANS as follows:

```
PROC SORT DATA=DEMO;
   BY SEX;

PROC MEANS DATA=DEMO;
   VAR BIRTHLGH BIRTHWGT;
   BY SEX;
```

But suppose you want a table printed with the individual lengths and weights, followed by the means. The PRINT procedure does not allow you to create a table with means of variables printed at the foot of each column. What we want to do is produce output like Exhibit 15.3, shown later in the chapter. An even simpler table which also cannot be obtained from a SAS procedure is Exhibit 15.2.

Such output is often referred to as a "customized report" since it is not produced by a standard program or SAS procedure. To produce such a report you need to process a sorted data set in a DATA step. The DATA step will use the PUT statement and special variables associated with the sorted data set. The special variables are used to control the process of summing a variable, counting the observations and, finally, computing the means.

THE FIRST. AND LAST.BYVARIABLES

When a sorted data set is input to a DATA step (by a SET statement), special variables, called FIRST. and LAST.byvariables are automatically created by the SAS System, provided the SET statement is followed by a BY statement specifying those variables by which the data set is sorted. For each such variable there are two byvariables: a FIRST.byvariable and a LAST.byvariable. Recall that when a data set is sorted it is, in effect, divided into groups (BY groups). The FIRST.byvariable is 1 (true) for the first observation in each BY group and 0 (false) for all other observations. The LAST.byvariable is 1 (true) for the last observation in each BY group and 0 (false) for all other observations.

When the data set is sorted on only one variable, there are only two byvariables. When the data set is sorted on several variables, there are two byvariables for each. Here is an example to show how this works. The following program inputs degree-days for three months for each of five cities, identified by CITY and PROVINCE.

```
DATA DEGDAY;
   INPUT CITY $ PROVINCE $ MONTH DEGDAY;
   LINES;
Winnipeg   Manitoba   1 666
Toronto    Ontario    1 716
Ottawa     Ontario    1 833
Montreal   Quebec     1 822
Quebec     Quebec     1 999
Winnipeg   Manitoba   2 777
Toronto    Ontario    2 432
Ottawa     Ontario    2 543
Montreal   Quebec     2 654
Quebec     Quebec     2 765
Winnipeg   Manitoba   3 567
Toronto    Ontario    3 333
Ottawa     Ontario    3 344
Montreal   Quebec     3 555
Quebec     Quebec     3 444
;

PROC SORT DATA=DEGDAY OUT=SORTPC;
   BY PROVINCE CITY;

DATA FIRSLAST;
   SET SORTPC;
     BY PROVINCE CITY;
   FIRSTP = FIRST.PROVINCE;
   LASTP = LAST.PROVINCE;
   FIRSTC = FIRST.CITY;
   LASTC = LAST.CITY;

TITLE 'Demonstration of FIRST. and LAST.byvariables';
PROC PRINT DATA=FIRSLAST;
   VAR PROVINCE CITY MONTH DEGDAY
      FIRSTP LASTP FIRSTC LASTC;
```

The data set is sorted by PROVINCE and CITY and then input to a DATA step. Note that the SET statement is followed by a BY statement specifying how the data set is sorted. The byvariables are only created if such a BY statement is included in the DATA step. The byvariables are called FIRST.PROVINCE and LAST.PROVINCE for the PROVINCE BY-groups and are called FIRST.CITY and LAST.CITY for the CITY BY-groups. In order to display these variables in PROC PRINT they have been assigned to new variables in the DATA step. The byvariables only exist for the duration of the DATA step and are not stored on the output data set (FIRSLAST in this case). The output from PROC PRINT is shown in Exhibit 15.1.

In the output you see that FIRSTP (= FIRST.PROVINCE) is 1 for the first observation for each of the provinces Manitoba, Ontario, and Quebec and is 0 for all other observations. Similarly, LASTP (= LAST.PROVINCE) is 1 for the last observation for each province and

---

Exhibit 15.1

```
              Demonstration of FIRST. and LAST.byvariables

    OBS PROVINCE CITY      MONTH DEGDAY FIRSTP LASTP FIRSTC LASTC

      1 Manitoba Winnipeg   1     666    1      0     1      0
      2 Manitoba Winnipeg   2     777    0      0     0      0
      3 Manitoba Winnipeg   3     567    0      1     0      1
      4 Ontario  Ottawa     1     833    1      0     1      0
      5 Ontario  Ottawa     2     543    0      0     0      0
      6 Ontario  Ottawa     3     344    0      0     0      1
      7 Ontario  Toronto    1     716    0      0     1      0
      8 Ontario  Toronto    2     432    0      0     0      0
      9 Ontario  Toronto    3     333    0      1     0      1
     10 Quebec   Montreal   1     822    1      0     1      0
     11 Quebec   Montreal   2     654    0      0     0      0
     12 Quebec   Montreal   3     555    0      0     0      1
     13 Quebec   Quebec     1     999    0      0     1      0
     14 Quebec   Quebec     2     765    0      0     0      0
     15 Quebec   Quebec     3     444    0      1     0      1
```

---

0 for all other observations. FIRSTC (= FIRST.CITY) is 1 five times since there are five cities and LASTC (= LAST.CITY) is 1 five times.

In the remaining sections of this chapter we will show how these byvariables are used for calculations and output.

PLANNING THE PROGRAM

In order to compute a mean of a variable, you initialize a sum and count to zero, count the number of observations, sum the variable over the observations, and, when you have reached the end of the observations, you compute the mean as the ratio of the sum to the count. If separate means are to be computed for each BY group, then this process must be carried out in each BY group separately. The byvariables identify when the BY group starts and ends. Hence, by testing for the values of the byvariables you can carry out the process for each BY group.

Here is the general plan of the DATA step. We assume that the data set is sorted by a variable GROUP. The main body of the DATA step is broken into three parts, one part executed only for the first observation of each BY group, one part executed for every observation of the BY group, and the last part executed only for the last observation of the BY group.

```
* code for first of BY group;
  IF FIRST.GROUP = 1 THEN DO;
     * initialize sum and count;
     * PUT headings for the group;
     END;
* code for every observation;
  * SUM statements to increment sum and count;
  * PUT statement to print observation (if desired);
* code for last of BY group;
  IF LAST.GROUP = 1 THEN DO;
     * calculate mean;
     * PUT mean for the group;
     END;
```

TWO EXAMPLES

Example 1

In this example we compute the mean degree-days for each of the five cities. The data were described earlier in the chapter. The data set is first sorted by CITY and then input to a DATA step by a SET statement followed by the same BY statement used for sorting. Notice that the DATA statement is DATA _NULL_;. When a DATA step has the sole purpose to create a customized report there is no need for it to create a SAS data set. The reserved word "_NULL_" is used instead of a data set name in the DATA statement.

The DATA step is divided into three parts, for the first observation, for every observation, and for the last observation.

```
PROC SORT DATA=DEGDAY OUT=SORTC;
  BY CITY;

TITLE;
DATA _NULL_;
  FILE PRINT;
  SET SORTC;
    BY CITY;
  * code for first of BY group;
    IF FIRST.CITY = 1 THEN DO;
      SUM = 0;
      COUNT = 0;
      END;
  * code for every observation;
    SUM + DEGDAY;
    COUNT + 1;
  * code for last of BY group;
    IF LAST.CITY = 1 THEN DO;
      MEAN = SUM/COUNT;
      PUT "Mean for " CITY "is " MEAN 5.1;
      PUT;
      END;
```

The output is shown in Exhibit 15.2.

Exhibit 15.2 Customized Report—Mean Degree Days

```
Mean for Montreal is 677.0

Mean for Ottawa is 573.3

Mean for Quebec is 736.0

Mean for Toronto is 493.7

Mean for Winnipeg is 670.0
```

Example 2

We return to the task suggested in the first paragraph of the chapter. We compute the mean birth lengths and weights for the two sexes in the Statlab data. The program follows the general plan outlined earlier. The only additional complications are: the sums must be computed for two variables, not just one; the length and weight are output for each observation; and more elaborate printed headings are programmed. The features used in the PUT statements are described in Chapter 10 and the formats in Chapter 12.

```
DATA DEMO;
  INFILE STATLAB;
  INPUT FAMILY $ SEX BLOOD BIRTHLGH BIRTHWGT TESTHGT
        TESTWGT LATERAL PEABODY RAVEN MOTHEDUC MOTHSMOK $;

PROC SORT DATA=DEMO OUT=SORTED;
  BY SEX;

TITLE;
DATA _NULL_;
  FILE PRINT;
  SET SORTED;
    BY SEX;
  * code for first of BY group;
    IF FIRST.SEX = 1 THEN DO;
      LGTHSUM = 0;
      WGHTSUM = 0;
      COUNT = 0;
      PUT @20 'Mean Lengths and Weights';
      PUT @27 'For sex = ' SEX;
      PUT @19 'Family' +4 'Length' +4 'Weight' OVERPRINT
          @19 '_____' +4 '_____' +4 '_____' ;
    END;
  * code for every observation;
    WGHTSUM + BIRTHWGT;
    LGTHSUM + BIRTHLGH;
    COUNT + 1;
    PUT @19 FAMILY +5 BIRTHLGH 4.1 +5 BIRTHWGT 4.1 ;
  * code for last of BY group;
    IF LAST.SEX = 1 THEN DO;
      AVGLG = LGTHSUM/COUNT;
      AVGWT = WGHTSUM/COUNT;
      PUT @29 '------' +4 '-----' ;
      PUT @18 'Means:' +6 AVGLG 5.2 +4 AVGWT 5.2 _PAGE_ ;
    END;
```

The output is shown in Exhibit 15.3.

Exhibit 15.3 Customized Report—Mean Lengths and Weights

```
              Mean Lengths and Weights
                    For sex = 1
              Family    Length    Weight
              41-21      20.5       6.9
              41-51      18.5       5.8
              42-21      20.0       8.5
              42-51      19.0       6.5
              43-21      22.0       8.3
                     .  .  .  .  .  .
              65-51      21.5       9.3
              66-21      21.0       9.5
              66-51      22.5       8.5
                        ------     -----
              Means:     20.47      7.57


              Mean Lengths and Weights
                    For sex = 2
              Family    Length    Weight
              11-21      21.0       7.1
              11-51      21.5       7.1
              12-21      22.0       9.7
              12-51      21.0       8.9
              13-21      20.0       6.4
                     .  .  .  .  .  .
              35-51      19.0       6.4
              36-21      19.5       6.5
              36-51      20.8       6.8
                        ------     -----
              Means:     20.51      7.52
```

Note: The ellipsis points (. . .) denote observations deleted to save space.

EXERCISES

1. Create output similar to Exhibit 15.1 for the sorted data sets of Chapter 13.

Part 4
EXTENDING THE SAS MODEL

The first three parts of this book have given us the basics of using the SAS System. In order to become more expert with the SAS language we have to have a good model of "how SAS works". Aspects of such a model are described in this part.

Chapter 16

THE SAS DATA SET

In Chapter 3, the structure of a SAS data set was briefly described. A SAS data set has two parts: a two-dimensional table and an index. The rows of the table are the observations and the columns are the variables; each entry in the table is the value of a variable for an observation. The index gives information about each variable, i.e., information about each column of the two-dimensional table.

In this chapter we discuss the index more thoroughly and show how information stored in the index can be used in PROC steps. In effect, this chapter describes how to modify and use information about the *columns* (variables) of the two-dimensional table. In the next chapter we discuss the *rows* (observations) of the table.

THE INDEX OF A SAS DATA SET

In Chapter 3, three characteristics of each variable were described. These were:

- the *column* the variable occupies in the two-dimensional table.
- the variable's *name*.
- the variable's *type* (numeric or character).

There are, in fact, five other characteristics stored in the index:

- the *length* of the variable specifies how much storage space is taken by the values of the variable. The default value for both numeric and character variables is 8 bytes (characters). This chapter reviews how to specify the length of a variable (previously discussed only for character variables in Chapter 7).
- the *label* of the variable is a string of up to 40 characters which can be used in procedures in addition to (or in place of) the variable's name as an identification of the variable. The label is stored in the index by a LABEL statement (see below).
- the *format* of the variable specifies value labels, i.e., labels for values or for groups of values of the variable. Formats were described in Chapter 12. In this chapter we show how permanently to associate a format with a variable.
- the *informat* of the variable specifies how the values of a variable are to be read by an INPUT statement. Informats are not discussed in this book.
- the *position* of the variable specifies the precise physical location of the variable in the data set. This information is rarely, if ever, needed by the user. In any case, the position cannot be changed by the user.

Of the eight characteristics of a variable which are stored in the index of a SAS data set, four (column, position, informat, and name) are not discussed further in this chapter. The column and position are handled for us automatically by the SAS System. Informats and how to change the name are not discussed in this book.

Four characteristics remain: type, length, label, and format. Each has a default value. In place of the default, a value may be specified for a variable by a SAS statement appearing in the DATA step which creates the data set. This value (or the default) is stored in the index of the data set and is used by succeeding DATA steps and PROC steps which process the data set. Alternatively, some of these characteristics can be defined temporarily in a PROC step. Information about these four characteristics is summarized in the following list and is explained in detail in the next four sections.

Type: Numeric or character

    Default   Numeric
    Defined by   INPUT, LENGTH, or assignment statement
    In PROC step   may not be changed

Length: Number of bytes

    Default   8 bytes
    Defined by   INPUT, LENGTH, or assignment statement
    In PROC step   may not be changed

Label: String up to 40 characters

    Default   null string
    Defined by   LABEL statement
    In PROC step   may be changed by LABEL statement

Format: Formatname

    Default   No format
    Defined by   FORMAT statement
    In PROC step   may be changed by FORMAT statement

The role of the SET statement

Many DATA steps take input from an existing SAS data set rather than from an external file. In such cases, the type, length, label, and format of the variables in the SAS data set are determined from the index to that data set. The type of a variable cannot be changed in the DATA step and an attempt to do so will be treated as an error by the SAS System. The length of a variable, already existing on an input SAS data set, can only be changed if the SET statement is *preceded* by a LENGTH statement. The label and format of existing variables can be changed by LABEL and FORMAT statements in the DATA step.

THE TYPE OF A VARIABLE

The type of a variable is determined by its first explicit or implicit mention in the DATA step which creates the data set. The variable can be mentioned explicitly in INPUT, LENGTH, and assignment statements. The variable can be mentioned implicitly if it is read by a SET statement. As previously noted, an attempt to change the type of a variable read by a SET statement is an error.

Determining type from INPUT or LENGTH statements

The variable's type is determined by whether a "$" follows the variable in an INPUT statement. Variables not followed by "$" are numeric; variables followed by "$" are character. Similarly, the "$" identifies character variables on a LENGTH statement. It is important to keep in mind that the type of a variable is set by its first appearance in a DATA step. It cannot be changed thereafter. Hence it is good practice always to have the LENGTH statement precede the INPUT statement and to have the character variables identified with "$" on the LENGTH statement.

Determining type from an assignment statement

A variable's first appearance in a DATA step may be in an assignment statement (although it is good practice to define the type of each variable by a preceding LENGTH statement). If the variable is on the left hand side, its type is the type of the expression on the right hand side. If the variable is on the right hand side it is assumed numeric and is given a missing value (since this is the first mention of the variable).[1]

THE LENGTH OF A VARIABLE

It takes a certain amount of space in a SAS data set to store the value of a variable.[2] This space is measured in bytes; the number of bytes is called the length of the variable. The default length is 8 bytes, for both numeric and character variables. We now describe why you might want to change the length and how you can do it. The considerations are somewhat different for character and numeric variables.

---

[1] See Chapter 6 for further details on missing values.

[2] We consider here only the space needed in the data set created by the DATA step. The value is also stored in the computer memory during the execution of the DATA step; somewhat different considerations then apply to the length of a variable (see Chapter 17).

Character variables

The length of a character variable is determined by its first explicit (INPUT, LENGTH, or assignment statement) or implicit (SET statement) mention in the DATA step which creates the data set. For details, see Chapter 7.

Numeric variables

For most applications, the default length of 8 bytes is appropriate. Unlike character variables, numeric variables of any size can be stored in 8 bytes since numbers are stored in scientific notation.[3] The length of a numeric variable can be set in the range from 2 to 8. (The only way to specify the length of a numeric variable is by a LENGTH statement.) The only situation in which you might consider shortening a numeric variable is when you are involved in a very large data processing application where the amount of space taken by the data set is critical. Such applications are beyond the scope of this book. It is suggested that the length of numeric variables never be changed from the default value of 8 as unexpected problems may arise if the length is shortened.[4]

VARIABLE LABELS

It is important to keep clear the distinction between variable labels and value labels. In Chapter 12 we showed how to assign labels to the *values* of a variable; e.g., the value 1 might have the label "Male", and the value 2 might have the label "Female". This association is done by a format (see next section). In this section we are describing how to assign a label to the *variable* itself; e.g., the variable SEX might have the label "Sex of the child".

Why are variable labels needed? Sometimes an eight (or fewer) character variable name is not sufficient to make output self-explanatory. In such cases, it is convenient to associate a label with the variable. In other cases, the variable names are not themselves meaningful, e.g., X1, X2, X3, etc. Associating labels with these arbitrary names overcomes this difficulty. The label is used in printed output. Most (but not all) procedures make use of a variable label, if defined. Most procedures display both the name and the label, but some, in particular PROC PRINT, use only the label.

Labels stored in the data set

Consider, for example, the following small example.[5] Suppose that variables X and Y represent errors and test score. These variables (and LASTN) may be given labels by the following DATA step:

---

[3] The range of numbers which can be stored depends on the computer but typically the numbers can range from 10^{-75} to 10^{+75}, approximately.

[4] See also Chapter 17 where it is noted that the length of numeric variables in the computer memory is always 8 bytes; the LENGTH statement for a numeric variable only affects the length of the variable in the SAS data set.

[5] Previously used in Exhibit 3.2.

```
DATA SCORES;
  INPUT X Y Z LASTN $ ;
  LABEL X = 'Number of errors'
        Y = 'Test score'
        LASTN = 'Last name';
  LINES;
23 46 5      Smith
  . . .
;
```

The labels are stored in the data set SCORES created by the DATA step and will be printed by most procedures which analyze the data set.

The general form of the LABEL statement is:

LABEL *variable* = '*label*' . . .;

Note that *label* must be enclosed in quotes and that *variable* is followed by an equals sign. Many variables may be given labels in one LABEL statement or, alternatively, each variable's label may be given in a separate LABEL statement. Labels can be up to 40 characters long (including blanks).

Labels defined in a PROC step

The LABEL statement may also be used in PROC steps. In this case, the labels are used only in that PROC step and override whatever labels, if any, exist in the index to the data set itself. For example, suppose the above DATA step were followed by this PROC step:

```
PROC UNIVARIATE DATA=TOY;
  VAR X Y Z;
  LABEL Y = 'Revised test score' Z = 'Time';
```

In the output from PROC UNIVARIATE, X would have the label "Number of errors" (from the data set), Y would have the label "Revised test score" (from the LABEL statement in the PROC step which overrides the label in the data set), and Z would have the label "Time" (from the PROC step).

How procedures use the label

The procedures CHART, FREQ, PLOT and UNIVARIATE print the variable label if it has been defined (either in the data set itself or by a LABEL statement in the PROC step). PROC MEANS uses the variable label if the line length is sufficient.[6] PROC SORT does not use the variable label (there is no printed output).

---

[6] The line is controlled by the SAS System option LINESIZE. See SAS Tip 1: *What you need to know about your computer system* in Chapter 1.

PROC PRINT can use variable labels but does not automatically do so. To use the variable labels you must use the option "LABEL" in the PROC PRINT statement. The option is required even if the label is defined by a LABEL statement in the PROC PRINT step itself. The PROC PRINT statement is then:

PROC PRINT DATA = *SASdataset* LABEL;

The reason that this option must be specified for PROC PRINT but not for any other procedure is that the labels will print as headings of columns in the output and this takes much more room than the variable names themselves. Requiring the LABEL option is essentially a safety measure to make sure you don't get a lot of extra output unless you really want it. If you do specify the LABEL option, the SAS System does its best to conserve space by splitting each label over several lines.

THE FORMAT OF A VARIABLE

The topic of formats was discussed thoroughly in Chapter 12. Formats are defined in a PROC FORMAT step and used in other PROC steps by associating the format name with a variable in a FORMAT statement. Only one addition need be made to the previous discussion. The association between variable and format name can be made *permanent* by including a FORMAT statement in the DATA step defining the variable. The format name is then stored in the index of the data step and that format is used by each procedure which analyzes that variable.

Formats are handled in a fashion similar to that of variable labels; hence the discussion of the preceding section need not be repeated in full. The only distinction which must be kept in mind is that it is really the "format name", not the format itself, which is analogous to a "label". The format must always be defined in a PROC FORMAT step (unless the format is pre-defined). This PROC FORMAT step must precede the DATA step or PROC step which includes the FORMAT statement which associates the format name and the variable. If the FORMAT statement appears in the DATA step, the association is permanent. If the FORMAT statement appears in the PROC step, then the association is temporary, just for that PROC step, and overrides whatever permanent association has been previously established. However, the permanent format name remains in the data set.

How procedures use the format

The procedures CHART, FREQ, PLOT and PRINT can make use of a format. Formats are not used in the analysis of continuous variables (which rules out procedures MEANS and UNIVARIATE) and are not used in sorting (ruling out PROC SORT).

In PROC CHART the variable on the horizontal axis can be grouped by a format. In procedures FREQ and PLOT, formatted values can be used for any of the variables. And in PROC PRINT the variable values are printed using the format. Examples of the use of formats in CHART, FREQ, and PRINT were shown in Chapter 12.

CHANGING THE VARIABLES IN A DATA SET

All variables which are mentioned in the DATA step are included in the data set which is created by the step. In more complex DATA steps it is often desirable to reduce the number of variables in the data set in order to save space or to make the writing of PROC steps more convenient. For example, PROC PRINT prints all the variables in a data set. If you want to print only a few variables you can do this by a VAR statement (probably the most natural way) or by creating the data set in the first place with only those variables you want to print; in the latter case you would not need a VAR statement.

The DROP statement gives a list of variables which are *not* to be included in the data set created by the DATA step. Its form is:

>   DROP *variables*;

You would use this statement if you had a large number of variables and only a few of them were to be excluded from the data set. On the other hand, if you are only including a few variables in the data set, it is easier to just list those variables you want to include. This is done by a KEEP statement:

>   KEEP *variables*;

The DROP or KEEP statement may appear anywhere in the DATA step. It is good practice to place it near the beginning of the step. Only one of these statements should be used in a given DATA step.

Example

When list input is used, all variables must be specified on the INPUT statement since there is no way to skip over fields in list input. In the following DATA step (without a DROP statement) the data set contains three variables: CODE, PROVINCE, and POP.

```
DATA PROVPOP;
   LENGTH PROVINCE $ 20;
   INPUT CODE $ PROVINCE & POP;
   LINES;
NF Newfoundland  0.57
PE Prince Edward Island  0.13
NS Nova Scotia  0.87
NB New Brunswick  0.71
PQ Quebec  6.54
ON Ontario  9.11
MB Manitoba  1.07
SK Saskatchewan  1.01
AB Alberta  2.38
BC British Columbia  2.89
;
```

In order to include only PROVINCE and POP in the data set, the DATA step would be changed to:

```
DATA PROVPOP;
   DROP CODE;
   LENGTH PROVINCE $ 20;
   INPUT CODE $ PROVINCE & POP;
   LINES;
   . . .
 ;
```

Instead of the DROP statement, the same effect could have been obtained by

```
KEEP PROVINCE POP;
```

Chapter 17

THE DATA STEP

In Chapter 16 we considered characteristics of the variables in a SAS data set. These characteristics (such as type, length, format) are stored in the index of the data set. The data values themselves are stored in the two-dimensional table, the columns of which represent the variables and the rows the observations. In Chapter 16 we focussed on the columns of the table. In this chapter we focus on the rows and the process which is carried out in the DATA step.

THE PROGRAM DATA VECTOR AND THE DATA-STEP PROCESS

Consider the following DATA step:

```
DATA CITY;
   LENGTH PLACE $ 12;
   INPUT PLACE A B C;
   LINES;
Toronto   5.67   -3.7   41567
Vancouver 4.53   2.8    11887
Regina    2.22   1.2    77267
   ;
```

This DATA step reads the lines following the LINES statement and creates the SAS data set CITY with four variables PLACE, A, B, and C, and one observation for each of the three lines. Let us now describe in more detail what happens during the DATA step.

When the SAS System begins a DATA step it sets up in computer memory a storage location for each variable mentioned in the DATA step. In the above case it would set up storage locations for the four variables. These storage locations form what is known as the *program data vector*. Each storage location can hold one value of the variable. The length of the storage location for numeric variables is always 8 bytes (regardless of any LENGTH specification[1]). The length of the storage location for character variables is 8 bytes (the default) unless the first mention of the variable in the DATA step indicates a different length. This means that if the character variable is first mentioned in a LENGTH statement the length is determined by that statement. Or if the character variable is first mentioned in an INPUT statement with column input then the length is determined by the field width specified by the columns on the INPUT statement. Note that if a LENGTH statement *followed* an INPUT statement with *list input* then the LENGTH statement would not have any effect since the length of a character variable is determined by the *first* mention of the variable.

The program data vector contains, for each variable, a storage location and a notation of the type and length of the variable. A representation of the program data vector which would be set up for the above DATA step is shown in Exhibit 17.1.

---

[1] See Chapter 16. The LENGTH statement, for numeric variables, only affects the space allocated to the variable on the output data set.

Exhibit 17.1 Program Data Vector

Name	Type	Length	Value												
PLACE	C	12													
A	N	8													
B	N	8													
C	N	8													

After setting up the program data vector, the SAS System begins a loop. In this loop, the SAS System reads one observation from a data line, stores the values from the data line in the program data vector, and then outputs one observation to the output data set, obtaining the values from the program data vector. This process is summarized in Exhibit 17.2 by a program written in "pseudo-code", i.e., by a program written in English. The description may seem unduly complicated for a very simple process. However, as we consider more complex DATA steps, we will see the need for even more detail.

We show, in Exhibit 17.3, the contents of the program data vector, for the above DATA step, at the end of each of the three cycles of the basic DATA-step process. In this exhibit, we have not shown explicitly the 8 bytes of each numeric variable since numbers are stored in those bytes in an internal representation which is not of interest to us. We simply show the number in its usual decimal form. However, we have shown explicitly the 12 bytes of the character variable.

Exhibit 17.2 Pseudo-code for the DATA Step—Short Version

- Set up program data vector (PDV) with one storage location for each variable appearing in (or brought into) the DATA step. Indicate for each variable its type and length (determined from first mention of variable, except that length of a numeric variable is always 8).

- DO WHILE (more observations)

  — Read one observation from instream data or from external file (following specification of INPUT statement) or from observation in data set (specified by SET) and store values of variables in PDV.

  — Output one observation to output data set. Use values from PDV but only include those variables specified by DROP/KEEP statements in DATA step or by DROP/KEEP options in DATA statement.

  — END (of DO WHILE)

- (Output data set complete; end of DATA step)

Exhibit 17.3 The Changing Program Data Vector

At End of First Cycle

Name	Value
PLACE	T o r o n t o
A	5.67
B	-3.7
C	41567

At End of Second Cycle

Name	Value
PLACE	V a n c o u v e r
A	4.53
B	2.8
C	11887

At End of Third Cycle

Name	Value
PLACE	R e g i n a
A	2.22
B	1.2
C	77267

MORE COMPLEX DATA STEPS

Most DATA steps have more statements than just the INPUT, SET, DROP, and KEEP statement covered by the pseudo-code in Exhibit 17.2. We show in Exhibits 17.4 and 17.5 a more complete description of the DATA-step process. A critical distinction is between those DATA steps with an INPUT or SET statement on the one hand and those DATA steps without such a statement. In the former DATA steps (Exhibit 17.4) an implicit loop cycles over observations in the input. In the latter DATA steps (Exhibit 17.5) there is no implicit loop. Cycling would occur only if there was an iterative DO loop.

Another critical distinction shown in both exhibits is the presence or absence of an OUTPUT statement in the DATA step. If there is an OUTPUT statement, there is no automatic output (to a SAS data set); all output is produced by the OUTPUT statement(s) in the DATA step. However, if there is no OUTPUT statement, then the output occurs automatically on each cycle of the implicit loop (or on the single pass if there is no INPUT or SET statement) unless the automatic output is bypassed by a subsetting IF, DELETE, or STOP statement.

Exhibit 17.4 Pseudo-code for DATA Steps with INPUT or SET Statements

- Set up program data vector (PDV) with one storage location for each variable appearing in (or brought into) the DATA step. Indicate for each variable its type and length (determined from first mention of variable, except that length of a numeric variable is always 8).

  Set values of input and assignment vars to missing.

  Set values of accumulator vars to zero.

- DO WHILE (more observations)

  — Set values of input and assignment vars (but not accumulator vars) to missing.

  — Read one observation from instream data or from external file (following specification of INPUT statement) or from observation in data set (specified by SET) and store values of variables in PDV.

  — Execute program statements, taking action shown below.

    - *Subsetting IF statement*: if condition *not* satisfied, jump to END (of DO WHILE) and hence continue with next observation.

    - *DELETE statement*: jump to END (of DO WHILE) and hence continue with next observation.

    - *STOP statement*: jump out of DO WHILE loop and hence output data set is complete.

    - *OUTPUT statement*: output one observation to output data set. Use values from PDV but only include those variables specified by DROP/KEEP statements in DATA step or by DROP/KEEP options in DATA statement.

    - *Other statement*: take appropriate action. (Includes assignment, iterative DO, IF-THEN/ELSE, and sum statements.)

  — IF (no OUTPUT statement in DATA step) THEN

    - Output one observation to output data set. Use values from PDV but only include those variables specified by DROP/KEEP statements in DATA step or by DROP/KEEP options in DATA statement.

  — END (of DO WHILE)

- (Output data set complete; end of DATA step)

Exhibit 17.5 Pseudo-code for DATA Steps without INPUT or SET Statements

- Set up program data vector (PDV) with one storage location for each variable appearing in the DATA step. Indicate for each variable its type and length (determined from first mention of variable, except that length of a numeric variable is always 8).

    Set values of assignment vars to missing.

    Set values of accumulator vars to zero.

- Execute program statements, taking action shown below.

    — *STOP statement*: jump to end of the DATA step and hence output data set is complete.

    — *OUTPUT statement*: output one observation to output data set. Use values from PDV but only include those variables specified by DROP/KEEP statements in DATA step or by DROP/KEEP options in DATA statement.

    — *Subsetting IF and DELETE statements*: these statements are not appropriate without SET or INPUT statements; if they occur the jump would be to the end of the DATA step.

    — *Other statement*: take appropriate action. (Includes assignment, iterative DO, IF-THEN/ELSE, and sum statements.) Since there are no SET or INPUT statements, looping (if any) must be explicitly programmed.

- IF (no OUTPUT statement in DATA step) THEN

    — Output one observation to output data set. Use values from PDV but only include those variables specified by DROP/KEEP statements in DATA step or by DROP/KEEP options in DATA statement.

- (Output data set complete; end of DATA step)

Appendix A

SAS STATEMENTS BY CHAPTER

The following conventions are used in the syntax specifications:

- Uppercase text is used exactly as shown.
- Lowercase italic text is replaced by appropriate text.
- Square bracketed text, [. . .], is optional.
- The word *options* should be read as if in square brackets.
- Ellipsis points, . . ., indicate that the preceding may be repeated.
- Vertical bar, |, means "or" (usually one or the other or both—the notation used here does not distinguish inclusive and exclusive or).

The specifications given here are sometimes written in a slightly different form than given in the chapter. See Appendix B for complete specifications (as covered in this book). The codes following some statements denote where the statements can be used (as described in that chapter):

-d- DATA step
-p- PROC step
-dp- either DATA or PROC step

PROC statements and statements associated with a PROC statement are not coded.

Chapter 2

Comment statement	-dp-

Chapter 3

DATA *SASdataset*;	-d-
INFILE *fileref*;	-d-
LINES;	-d-
Null statement	-d-
INPUT *specification*;	-d-
specification: *List input* | *Column input*	

Chapter 4

PROC *procedure* DATA = *SASdataset*;	
PROC PRINT DATA = *SASdataset*;	
VAR *variables*;	
ID *variables*;	
SUM *variables*;	
TITLE '*title*';	-dp-
TITLE*n* '*title*';	-dp-

PROC CHART DATA = *SASdataset*;
  VBAR *variables* | *options*;
    options: TYPE = *type* | DISCRETE | MIDPOINTS = *values* | LEVELS = *n*
    type: FREQ | PERCENT | CFREQ | CPERCENT
PROC PLOT DATA = *SASdataset*;
  PLOT *requests* | *options*;
    requests: *vertical*horizontal* |
            vertical*horizontal = '*character*' |
            vertical*horizontal = *variable*
    options: VAXIS = *values* | HAXIS = *values* |
         VREF = *values* | HREF = *values* |
        OVERLAY

Chapter 5

PROC MEANS DATA = *SASdataset options*;
    options: MAXDEC = *n* | *statistics*
    statistics: N | MEAN | STD | MIN | MAX | RANGE | SUM | VAR |
           SKEWNESS | KURTOSIS
  VAR *variables*;
PROC UNIVARIATE DATA = *SASdataset*;
  VAR *variables*;
PROC FREQ DATA = *SASdataset*;
  TABLES *requests* | *options*;
    requests: *variable* | *variable*variable*
    options: NOFREQ | NOPERCENT | NOROW | NOCOL
PROC CHART DATA = *SASdataset*;
  VBAR *variables* | *options*;
    options: TYPE = *type* | SUMVAR = *variable* |
        GROUP = *variable* | SUBGROUP = *variable* |
        DISCRETE | MIDPOINTS = *values* | LEVELS = *n*
    type: FREQ | PERCENT | CFREQ | CPERCENT | MEAN | SUM

Chapter 6

Assignment statement   -d-
Sum statement   -d-

Chapter 7

LENGTH *variables* [$] *length* . . .;   -d-

Chapter 8

IF *condition* THEN *statement*$_1$;   -d-
  ELSE *statement*$_2$;
DO;   -d-
END;   -d-

Chapter 9

SET *SASdataset*;   -d-
INPUT *specification*;   -d-
    specification: *List input | Column input | & | @n | + n | #n | / | @@*
INFILE *fileref options*;   -d-
    options: FIRSTOBS = *linenumber* | OBS = *linenumber*

Chapter 10

FILE *fileref*;   -d-
PUT *specification*;   -d-
    specification: *List style | Column style | Named output |*
                      @n | + n | #n | / | _PAGE_ | OVERPRINT
DATA *SASdataset* . . .;   -d-
OUTPUT [*SASdataset*] . . .;   -d-
INFILE *fileref* [END = *endvariable*];   -d-
SET *SASdataset* [END = *endvariable*];   -d-
IF *condition*;   -d-
DELETE statement   -d-
STOP statement   -d-

Chapter 11

DO *indexvariable* = *start* TO *stop* [BY *increment*];   -d-
END;   -d-

Chapter 12

PROC FORMAT;
  VALUE *formatname range* = '*label*' *range* = '*label*' . . .;
FORMAT *variables formatname* . . .;   -dp-
PUT *specification*;   -d-
    specification: *Formatted style*

Chapter 13

PROC SORT DATA = *SASdataset* [OUT = *SASdataset*];
  BY [DESCENDING] *variable* . . .;

Chapter 14

BY [DESCENDING] *variable* . . .;   -p-

Chapter 15

BY [DESCENDING] *variable* . . .;   -d-

Chapter 16

LABEL *variable* = '*label*' . . .;   -dp-
PROC PRINT DATA = *SASdataset options*;
    options: LABEL
DROP *variables*;   -d-
KEEP *variables*;   -d-

Appendix B

INDEX TO SAS STATEMENTS

See Appendix A for syntax conventions used. The numbers listed to the right are the numbers of the chapters in which the statement is discussed. For more precise locations, see the Index.

DATA step

Assignment statement	6
BY [DESCENDING] *variable* . . .;	15
Comment statement	2
DATA *SASdataset* . . .;	3, 10
DELETE statement;	10
DO;	8
DO *indexvariable* = *start* TO *stop* [BY *increment*];	11
DROP *variables*;	16
END;	8, 11
FILE *fileref*;	10
FORMAT *variables formatname* . . .;	12, 16
IF *condition*;	10
IF *condition* THEN *statement*$_1$;	8
ELSE *statement*$_2$;	
INFILE *fileref options*;	3, 9, 10
options: END = *endvariable* | FIRSTOBS = *linenumber* | OBS = *linenumber*	
INPUT *specification*;	3, 9
specification: List input | Column input | & | @*n* | +*n* | #*n* | / | @@	
KEEP *variables*;	16
LABEL *variable* = ' *label*' . . .;	16
LENGTH *variables* [$] *length* . . .;	7, 16
LINES;	3
Null statement	3
OUTPUT [*SASdataset*] . . .;	10, 11
PUT *specification*;	10, 12
specification: List style | Column style | Named output | Formatted style |	
@*n* | +*n* | #*n* | / | _PAGE_ | OVERPRINT	
SET *SASdataset* [END = *endvariable*];	9, 10
STOP statement;	10
Sum statement	6
TITLE ' *title*';	4
TITLE*n* ' *title*';	4

PROC step

Statements used in any PROC step

INDEX